The Canadian's Guide to Investing

by Tony Martin, BCom
and Eric Tyson, MBA

WILEY

Publisher's Acknowledgments

Authors: Tony Martin, BCom and Eric Tyson, MBA

Senior Acquisitions Editor: Tracy Boggier

Project Manager: Elizabeth Kuball

Compilation Editor: Georgette Beatty

Production Editor: Mohammed Zafar Ali

Cover Photo: © mingcreative/ Getty Images, © stockish/ Shutterstock

The Canadian's Guide to Investing

Published by John Wiley & Sons, Inc.
111 River St.
Hoboken, NJ 07030-5774
http://www.wiley.com

Copyright © 2019 by Eric Tyson and Tony Martin

For general information on our other products and services, please contact our Business Development Department in the U.S. at 317-572-3205.

Library of Congress Control Number: 2019942821

ISBN 978-1-119-60995-7 (pbk)

Manufactured in the United States of America

V10011159_061319

Table of Contents

1

Weighing Risks and Returns

A woman passes up eating a hamburger at a picnic because she heard that she could contract a deadly *E. coli* infection from eating improperly cooked meat. The next week, that same woman hops in the passenger seat of her friend's old model car that lacks airbags.

This isn't meant to depress or frighten anyone. This is to make an important point about risk — something everyone deals with on a daily basis. Risk is in the eye of the beholder. Many people base their perception of risk, in large part, on their experiences and what they've been exposed to. In doing so, they often fret about relatively small risks while overlooking much larger risks.

In the world of investing, most folks worry about certain risks — some of which may make sense and some of which may not — but at the same time they completely overlook or disregard other, more significant risks. This chapter discusses a range of investments and their risks and expected returns.

Different Types of Risks

Everywhere you turn, risks exist; some are just more apparent than others. Many people misunderstand risks. With increased knowledge, you may be able to reduce or conquer some of your fears and make more sensible decisions about reducing risks.

For example, some people who fear flying don't understand that statistically, flying is much safer than driving a car. You're approximately 110 times more likely to die in a motor vehicle than in an airplane. But when a plane goes down, it's big news because dozens and sometimes hundreds of people, who weren't engaging in reckless behaviour, perish. Meanwhile, the national media seem to pay less attention to the 100 people, on average, who die on the road every day.

Then there's the issue of control. Flying seems more dangerous to some folks because the pilots are in control of the plane, whereas in your car, you can at least be at the steering wheel. Of course, you can't control what happens around you or mechanical problems with the mode of transportation you're using.

This doesn't mean that you shouldn't drive or fly or that you shouldn't drive to the airport. However, you may consider steps you can take to reduce the significant risks you expose yourself to in a car. For example, you can get a car with more safety features, or you can bypass riding with reckless taxi drivers.

Although some people like to live life to its fullest and take "fun" risks (how else can you explain mountain climbers, parachutists, and bungee jumpers?), most people seek to minimize risk and maximize enjoyment in their lives. The vast majority of people also understand that they'd be a lot less happy living a life in which they sought to eliminate all risks, and they likely wouldn't be able to do so anyway.

Likewise, if you try to avoid all the risks involved in investing, you likely won't succeed, and you likely won't be happy with your investment results and lifestyle. In the investment world, some people don't go near stocks or any investment that they perceive to be volatile. As a result, such investors often end up with lousy long-term returns and expose themselves to some high risks that they overlooked, such as the risk of having inflation and taxes erode the purchasing power of their money.

You can't live without taking risks. Risk-free activities or ways of living don't exist. You can minimize but never eliminate risks. Some methods of risk reduction aren't palatable because they reduce your quality of life. Risks are also composed of several factors. The following sections discuss the various types of investment risks and go over proven methods you can use to sensibly reduce these risks while not missing out on the upside that growth investments offer.

Market value risk

Although the stock market can help you build wealth, most people recognize that it can also drop substantially — by 10 percent, 20 percent, or 30 percent (or more) in a relatively short period of time. After peaking in 2000, Canadian and U.S. stocks, as measured by the major indexes representing the value of large companies (for Canada, the S&P/TSX Composite Index, and for the United States, the S&P 500 index), dropped about 50 percent by 2002. Stocks on the Nasdaq, which is heavily weighted toward technology stocks, plunged more than 76 percent from 2000 through 2002!

After a multiyear rebound, stocks peaked in 2007 and then dropped sharply during the financial crisis of 2008. From peak to bottom, Canadian, U.S., and global stocks dropped by some 50 percent or more.

In a mere six weeks (from mid-July 1998 to early September 1998), large-company Canadian and U.S. stocks fell about 20 percent. An index of smaller-company U.S. stocks dropped 33 percent over a slightly longer period of two and a half months.

If you think that the stock market crash that occurred in the fall of 1987 was a big one (the market plunged by about a third in a matter of weeks), take a look at Tables 1-1 and 1-2, which list major declines over the past 100-plus years that were all *worse* than the 1987 crash. Note that two of these major declines happened in the 2000s: 2000 to 2002 and 2007 to 2009.

Period	Size of Fall
1929–1932	80% (ouch!)
1937–1942	56%
2000–2002	50%
2007–2009	48%
1980–1982	44%
1973–1974	38%
1987–1987	31%
1956–1957	30%
1969–1970	28%

Table 1-1: *Most Depressing Canadian Stock Market Declines*
* As measured by changes in the TSE/TSX composite index

Real estate exhibits similar unruly, annoying tendencies. Although real estate (like stocks) has been a terrific long-term investment, various real estate markets get clobbered from time to time.

Period	Size of Fall
1929–1932	89% (ouch!)
2007–2009	55%
1937–1942	52%
1906–1907	49%
1890–1896	47%
1919–1921	47%
1901–1903	46%
1973–1974	45%
1916–1917	40%
2000–2002	39%

Table 1-2: *Largest U.S. Stock Market Declines*
* As measured by changes in the Dow Jones Industrial Average

When the oil industry collapsed in Alberta in the early 1980s, real estate prices in the province dropped by 25 percent. And after a massive run-up in prices in the mid-1980s, house prices in the Toronto area plummeted by nearly 28 percent over the next few years. Across Canada, after a whopping 50 percent rise from 1978 to 1981, house prices dropped by 35 percent in just over a year. Then, after hitting a new high in 1990, the market fell by 15 percent in just 12 months, and by 1996 it was down 22 percent.

In the United States, housing prices took a 25 percent tumble from the late 1920s to the mid-1930s. Later, in the 1980s and early 1990s, the northeastern United States became mired in a severe recession, and real estate prices fell by 20-plus percent in many areas. After peaking near 1990, many of the West Coast housing markets, especially those in California, experienced falling prices — dropping 20 percent or more in most areas by the mid-1990s.

Declining U.S. housing prices in the mid- to late 2000s garnered unprecedented attention. Some folks and pundits acted like it was the worst housing market ever. Foreclosures increased in part because of buyers who financed their home purchases with risky mortgages. But note that housing market conditions also vary tremendously by area. For example, housing prices in Toronto and Vancouver have often shown double-digit increases while smaller cities and towns were experiencing down markets. In the United States, some portions of the Pacific Northwest and South actually appreciated during the mid- to late 2000s, while other U.S. markets experienced substantial declines.

After reading this section, you may want to keep all your money in the bank — after all, you know you won't lose your money, and you won't have to be a nonstop worrier. Since the Canadian Deposit Insurance Corporation (CDIC) came into existence, which protects deposits at banks and trust companies up to $100,000, people don't lose 20 percent, 40 percent, 60 percent, or 80 percent of their bank-held savings vehicles within a few years, but major losses prior to then did happen. Just keep in mind, though, that just letting your money sit around would be a mistake.

If you pass up the stock and real estate markets simply because of the potential market value risk, you miss out on a historic, time-tested method of building substantial wealth. Instead of seeing declines and market corrections as horrible things, view them as potential opportunities or "sales." Try not to give in to the human emotions that often scare people away from buying something that others seem to be shunning.

Later in this chapter, you see the generous returns that stocks and real estate, as well as other investments, have historically provided. The following sections suggest some simple things you can do to lower your investing risk and help prevent your portfolio from suffering a huge fall.

Diversify for a gentler ride

If you worry about the health of the economy, the government, and the dollar, you can reduce your investment risk by investing outside of Canada. Most large Canadian companies do business in the United States and overseas, so when you invest in larger Canadian company stocks, you get some international investment exposure. You can also invest in international company stocks, ideally via mutual funds and exchange-traded funds (see Chapter 5).

Of course, investing overseas can't totally protect you in the event of a global economic catastrophe. If you worry about the risk of such a calamity, you should probably also worry about a huge meteor crashing into Earth.

Diversifying your investments can involve more than just your stock portfolio. You can also hold some real estate investments to diversify your investment portfolio. Many real estate markets appreciated in the early 2000s while North American stock markets were in the doghouse. Conversely, when real estate in many regions entered a multiyear slump in the mid-2000s, stocks performed well during that period. In the late 2000s, stock prices fell sharply while real estate prices in many major centres rose, but then stocks came roaring back.

Consider your time horizon

Investors who worry that the stock market may take a dive and take their money down with it need to consider the length of time that they plan to invest. In a one-year period in the stock and bond markets, a wide range of outcomes can occur. History shows that you lose money about once in every three years that you invest in the stock and bond markets. However, stock market investors have made money (sometimes substantial amounts) approximately two-thirds of the time over a one-year period. (Bond investors made money about two-thirds of the time, too, although they made a good deal less on average.)

Although the stock market is more volatile than the bond market in the short term, stock market investors have earned far better long-term returns than bond investors have. (See the later section "Stock returns" for details.) Why? Because stock investors bear risks that bond investors don't bear, and they can reasonably expect to be compensated for those risks. Keep in mind, however, that bonds generally outperform a boring old bank account.

History has shown that the risk of a stock or bond market fall becomes less of a concern the longer you plan to invest. As the holding period for owning stocks increases from 1 year to 3 years to 5 years to 10 years and then to 20 years, there's a greater likelihood of seeing stocks increase in value. In fact, over any 20-year time span, the U.S. stock market, as measured by the S&P 500 Index of larger company stocks, has *never* lost money, even after you subtract the effects of inflation.

Since 1957, only one five-year period in Canada has had a negative return. In other words, if you had invested in the broad market (meaning your returns were similar to the composite index) and held on for five years, in only one period would you have had less after five years than you started with. If you had invested and *stayed* invested for ten years, you would have always come out ahead. To put it another way, starting in 1957, if you had invested in any year and held those investments for a minimum of ten years, you would always have ended up with a profit, assuming your returns matched those of the index.

Most stock market investors are concerned about the risk of losing money. The key to minimizing the probability that you'll lose money in stocks is to hold them for the longer term. Don't invest in stocks unless you plan to hold them for at least five years — and preferably a decade or longer. Check out Chapters 3 and 5 for more on using stocks as a long-term investment.

Pare down holdings in bloated markets

Perhaps you've heard the expression "buy low, sell high." Although you can't *time the markets* (that is, predict the most profitable time to buy and sell), spotting a greatly overpriced or underpriced market isn't too difficult. This book explains some simple yet powerful methods you can use to measure whether a particular investment market is of fair value, of good value, or overpriced. You should avoid overpriced investments for two important reasons:

- If — and when — these overpriced investments fall, they usually fall farther and faster than more fairly priced investments.

- You should be able to find other investments that offer higher potential returns.

Ideally, you want to avoid having a lot of your money in markets that appear overpriced (see Chapter 3 for how to spot pricey markets). Practically speaking, avoiding overpriced markets doesn't mean that you should try to sell all your holdings in such markets with the vain hope of buying them back at a much lower price. However, you may benefit from the following strategies:

- **Invest new money elsewhere.** Focus your investment of new money somewhere other than the overpriced market; put it into investments that offer you better values. As a result, without selling any of your seemingly expensive investments, you make them a smaller portion of your total holdings. If you hold investments outside of tax-sheltered plans, focusing your money elsewhere also allows you to avoid incurring taxes from selling appreciated investments.

- **If you have to sell, sell the expensive stuff.** If you need to raise money to live on, such as for retirement or for a major purchase, sell the pricier holdings. As long as the taxes aren't too troublesome, it's better to sell high and lock in your profits.

Individual investment risk

A downdraft can put an entire investment market on a roller-coaster ride, but healthy markets also have their share of individual losers. For example, from the early 1980s through the late 1990s, Canadian and U.S. stock markets had one of the greatest appreciating markets in history. You'd never know it, though, if you held one of the great losers of that period.

Consider a company now called Navistar, which has undergone enormous transformations in recent decades. This company used to be called International Harvester, and it manufactured farm equipment, trucks, and construction and other industrial equipment. Today, Navistar makes mostly trucks.

In late 1983, the company's stock traded at more than US$140 per share. It then plunged more than 90 percent over the ensuing decade. Even with a rally in recent years, Navistar stock still trades at less than US$20 per share at the time of writing (after dipping below US$10 per share). Lest you think that's a big drop, the company's stock traded as high as US$455 per share in the late 1970s. If a worker retired from the company in the late 1970s with $200,000 invested in the company stock, the retiree's investment would be worth about $6,000 today. On the other hand, if the retiree had simply swapped his stock at retirement for a diversified portfolio of stocks (see Chapter 5), his $200,000 nest egg would've instead grown to more than $5 million.

Like most other markets, the Canadian stock market paled by comparison with the U.S. juggernaut in the 1990s, but this country has had its share of stocks that have plummeted in value. How about Dylex, which through its many brand-name outlets, such as Suzy Shier, at one time took in one out of every ten dollars consumers spent in retail clothing outlets? The stock, which began the 1990s at $24, ended the decade languishing beneath the $10 mark, dwindling lower and lower until the company eventually went under in 2001.

Just as individual stock prices can plummet, so can individual real estate property prices. In California during the 1990s, for example, earthquakes rocked the prices of properties built on landfills. These quakes highlighted the dangers of building on poor soil. In the decade prior, real estate values in the communities of Times Beach, Missouri, and Love Canal, New York, plunged because of carcinogenic toxic waste contamination. (Ultimately, many property owners in these areas received compensation for their losses from the federal government, as well as from some real estate agencies that didn't disclose these known contaminants.)

 Here are some simple steps you can take to lower the risk of individual investments that can upset your goals:

- **Do your homework.** When you purchase real estate, a whole host of inspections can save you from buying a money pit. With stocks, you can examine some measures of value and the company's financial condition and business strategy to reduce your chances of buying into an overpriced company or one on the verge of major problems.

- **Diversify.** Investors who seek growth invest in securities such as stocks. Placing significant amounts of your capital in one or a handful of securities is risky, particularly if the stocks are in the same industry or closely related industries. To reduce this risk, purchase stocks in a variety of industries and companies within each industry.

- **Hire someone to invest for you.** The best funds (see Chapter 5) offer low-cost, professional management and oversight as well as diversification. Stock funds typically own 25 or more securities in a variety of companies in different industries. You can invest in real estate in a similar way (that is, by leaving the driving to someone else).

Purchasing power risk (also known as inflation risk)

Inflation (increases in the cost of living) can erode the value of your retirement resources and what you can buy with that money — also known as its *purchasing power*. Here's an example: When Teri retired at the age of 60, she was pleased with her retirement income. She was receiving an $800-per-month pension and $1,200 per month from money that she had invested in long-term bonds. Her monthly expenditures amounted to about $1,500, so she was able to save a little money for an occasional trip.

Fast-forward 15 years. Teri still receives $800 per month from her pension, but now she gets only $900 per month of investment income, which comes from some certificates of deposit. Teri bailed out of bonds after she lost sleep over the sometimes roller-coaster-like price movements in the bond market. Her monthly expenditures now amount to approximately $2,400, and she uses some of her investment principal (original investment). She's terrified of outliving her money.

Teri has reason to worry. She has 100 percent of her money invested without protection against increases in the cost of living. Although her income felt comfortable in the beginning of her retirement, it doesn't at age 75, and Teri may easily live another 15 or more years.

The erosion of the purchasing power of your investment dollar can, over longer time periods, be as bad as or worse than the effect of a major market crash. Table 1-3 shows the effective loss in purchasing power of your money at various rates of inflation and over differing time periods.

Skittish investors have tried to keep their money in bonds and money market accounts, thinking they were playing it safe. The risk in this strategy is that your money won't grow enough over the years for you to accomplish your financial goals. In other words, the lower the return you earn, the more you need to save to reach a particular financial goal.

Inflation Rate	10 Years	15 Years	25 Years	40 Years
2%	–18%	–26%	–39%	–55%
4%	–32%	–44%	–62%	–81%
6%	–44%	–58%	–77%	–90%
8%	–54%	–68%	–85%	–95%
10%	–61%	–76%	–91%	–98%

Table 1-3: *Inflation's Corrosive Effect on Your Money's Purchasing Power*

A 40-year-old wanting to accumulate $500,000 by age 65 would need to save $722 per month if she earns a 6 percent average annual return, but she needs to save only $377 per month if she earns a 10 percent average return per year. Younger investors need to pay the most attention to the risk of generating low returns, but so should younger senior citizens. Even by the age of 65, seniors need to recognize that a portion of their assets may not be used for a decade or more from the present.

Career risk

Your ability to earn money is most likely your single biggest asset or at least one of your biggest assets. Most people achieve what they do in the working world through education and hard work. Education doesn't simply mean what one learns in formal schooling. Education is a lifelong process. People have learned far more about business from their own frontline experiences and those of others, as well as training others, than they've learned in educational settings. Reading a lot also helps.

If you don't continually invest in your education, you risk losing your competitive edge. Your skills and perspectives can become dated and obsolete. Although that doesn't mean you should work 80 hours a week and never do anything fun, it does mean that part of your "work" time should involve upgrading your skills.

The best organizations are those that recognize the need for continual knowledge and invest in their workforce through training and career development. Just be sure to look at your own career objectives, which may not be the same as your company's.

How to Analyze Returns

When you make investments, you have the potential to make money in a variety of ways. Each type of investment has its own mix of associated risks that you take when you part with your investment dollar and, likewise, offers a different potential rate of return. The following sections cover the returns you can expect with each of the common investing avenues. But first, you go through the components of calculating the total return on an investment.

The components of total return

To figure out exactly how much money you've made (or lost) on your investment, you need to calculate the *total return*. To come up with this figure, you need to determine how much money you originally invested and then factor in the other components, such as interest, dividends, and appreciation (or depreciation).

If you've ever had money in a bank account that pays interest, you know that the bank pays you a small amount of interest when you allow it to keep your money. The bank then turns around and lends your money to some other person or organization at a much higher rate of interest. The rate of interest is also known as the *yield*. So, if a bank tells you that its savings account pays 2 percent interest, the bank may also say that the account yields 2 percent. Banks usually quote interest rates or yields on an annual basis. Interest that you receive is one component of the return you receive on your investment.

If a bank pays monthly interest, the bank also likely quotes a *compounded effective annual yield*. After the first month's interest is credited to your account, that interest starts earning interest as well. So, the bank may say that the account pays 2 percent, which then compounds to an effective annual yield of 2.04 percent.

When you lend your money directly to a company — which is what you do when you invest in a bond that a corporation or a government issues — you also receive interest.

Bonds, as well as stocks (which are shares of ownership in a company), fluctuate in value after they're issued.

When you invest in a company's stock, you hope that the stock *appreciates* (increases) in value. Of course, a stock can also *depreciate* (decrease) in value. This change in market value is part of your return from a stock or bond investment:

(Current investment value – Original investment) ÷ Original investment = Appreciation or depreciation

For example, if one year ago you invested $10,000 in a stock (you bought 1,000 shares at $10 per share) and the investment is now worth $11,000 (each share is worth $11), your investment's appreciation looks like this:

($11,000 – $10,000) ÷ $10,000 = 10

Stocks can also pay *dividends,* which are the company's sharing of some of its profits with you as a shareholder. Some companies, particularly those that are small or growing rapidly, choose to reinvest all their profits back into the company. (Of course, some companies don't turn a profit, so they don't have anything to pay out.) You need to factor any dividends into your return as well.

Suppose that in the previous example, in addition to your stock appreciating from $10,000 to $11,000, it paid you a dividend of $100 ($1 per share). Here's how you calculate your total return:

([Current investment value − Original investment] + Dividends) ÷ Original investment = Total return

You can apply this formula to the example like so:

([$11,000 − $10,000] + $100) ÷ $10,000 = 11

After-tax returns

Although you may be happy that your stock has given you an 11 percent return on your invested dollars, note that unless you held your investment in a tax-deferred Registered Retirement Savings Plan (RRSP), registered retirement plan, Registered Education Savings Plan (RESP), or Tax-Free Savings Account (TFSA), you owe taxes on your return. Specifically, the dividends and investment appreciation that you realize upon selling are taxed, although often at relatively low rates. The tax rates on so-called long-term capital gains and stock dividends are lower than the tax rates on other income. Chapter 2 discusses the different tax rates that affect your investments and explains how to make tax-wise investment decisions that fit with your overall personal financial situation and goals.

If you've invested in savings accounts, money market accounts, or bonds outside of a tax-deferred registered retirement plan or a TFSA, you owe the Canada Revenue Agency (CRA) taxes on the interest.

Often, people make investing decisions without considering the tax consequences of their moves. This is a big mistake. What good is making money if the government takes away a substantial portion of it?

If you're in a moderate tax bracket, taxes on your investment probably run in the neighborhood of 30 percent (federal and provincial). So, if your investment returned 6 percent before taxes, you're left with a net return of about 4.2 percent after taxes.

Psychological returns

Profits and tax avoidance can powerfully motivate your investment selections. However, as with other life decisions, you need to consider more than the bottom line. Some people want to have fun with their investments. Of course, they don't want to lose money or sacrifice a lot of potential returns. Fortunately, less expensive ways to have fun do exist.

Psychological rewards compel some investors to choose particular investment vehicles such as individual stocks, real estate, or a small business. Why? Because compared with other investments, such as managed mutual funds and exchange-traded funds, they see these investments as more tangible and, well, more fun.

Be honest with yourself about why you choose the investments that you do. Allowing your ego to get in the way can be dangerous. Do you want to invest in individual stocks because you really believe that you can do better than the best full-time professional money managers? Chances are, you won't. Such questions are worth considering as you contemplate which investments you want to make.

Savings, high-interest, and money market account returns

You need to keep your extra cash that awaits investment (or an emergency) in a safe place, preferably one that doesn't get hammered by the sea of changes in the financial markets. By default and for convenience, many people keep their extra cash in a bank savings account. Although the bank offers the backing of the Canadian Deposit Insurance Corporation (CDIC), it comes at a price. Most banks pay a relatively low interest rate on their savings accounts.

A far better place to keep your liquid savings are the growing number of high-interest savings accounts offered by companies such as Alterna Bank, DUCA Credit Union, or Tangerine, and now most mutual fund companies and big banks as well. These accounts typically offer rates anywhere from 4 to 40 — yes, 40 — times the rate on savings accounts.

Another good place to keep your liquid savings is in a money market mutual fund. These are the safest types of mutual funds around and, for all intents and purposes, equal a bank savings account's safety. The best money market funds generally pay higher yields than most bank savings accounts. Unlike a bank, money market mutual funds tell you how much they deduct for the service of managing your money.

If you don't need immediate access to your money, consider using Treasury bills (T-bills) or Guaranteed Investment Certificates (GICs), which are usually issued for terms of anywhere from three months to five years. Your money will generally earn more in one of these vehicles than in a bank savings account. (In recent years, the yields on T-bills have been so low that the best CDIC-insured bank savings accounts have higher yields.) Rates vary by institution, so it's essential to shop around. The drawback to T-bills and GICs is that you incur a penalty (with GICs) or a transaction fee (with T-bills) if you withdraw your investment before the term expires (see Chapter 4).

You may be wondering, "What does the phrase *liquid savings* mean?" The term *liquidity* refers to how long and at what cost it takes to convert an investment into cash:

- The money in your wallet is considered perfectly liquid — it's already cash.
- Suppose that you invested money in a handful of stocks. Although you can't easily sell these stocks on a Saturday night, you can sell most stocks quickly through a broker for a nominal fee any day that the financial markets are open (normal working days).

You pay a higher percentage to sell your stocks if you use a high-cost broker or if you have a small amount of stock to sell.

- Real estate is generally much less liquid than stock. Preparing your property for sale takes time, and if you want to get fair market value for your property, finding a buyer may take weeks or months. Selling costs (agent commissions, fix-up expenses, and closing costs) can approach 8 percent to 10 percent of the home's value.

- A privately run small business is among the least liquid of the better growth investments that you can make. Selling such a business typically takes longer than selling most real estate.

Bond returns

When you buy a bond, you lend your money to the issuer of that bond (borrower), which is generally the federal government, a provincial government, or a corporation, for a specific period of time. When you buy a bond, you expect to earn a higher yield than you can with a money market or savings account. You're taking more risk, after all. Companies can and do go bankrupt, in which case you may lose some or all of your investment.

Generally, you can expect to earn a higher yield when you buy bonds that

- **Are issued for a longer term:** The bond issuer is tying up your money at a fixed rate for a longer period of time.
- **Have lower credit quality:** The bond issuer may not be able to repay the principal.

Wharton School of Business professor Jeremy Siegel has tracked the performance of bonds and stocks back to 1802. Although you may say that what happened in the 19th century has little relevance to the financial markets and economy of today, the decades since the Great Depression of the 1930s, which most other return data track, are a relatively small slice of time.

Note that although the rate of inflation has increased since the Great Depression, bond returns haven't increased over the decades, according to the data. Long-term bonds maintained slightly higher returns in recent years than short-term bonds. The bottom line: Bond investors typically earn about 4 percent to 5 percent per year.

Stock returns

Investors expect a fair return on their investments. If one investment doesn't offer a seemingly high enough potential rate of return, investors can choose to move their money into other investments that they believe will perform better. Instead of buying a diversified basket of stocks and holding, some investors frequently buy and sell, hoping to cash in on the latest hot investment. This tactic seldom works in the long run.

Unfortunately, some of these investors use a rearview mirror when they purchase their stocks, chasing after investments that have recently performed strongly on the assumption (and the hope) that those investments will continue to earn good returns. But chasing after the strongest-performing investments can be dangerous if you catch the stock at its peak, ready to begin a downward spiral. You may have heard that the goal of investing is to buy low and sell high. Chasing high-flying investments can lead you to buy high, with the prospect of having to sell low if the stock runs out of steam. Even though stocks as a whole have proved to be a good long-term investment, picking individual stocks is a risky endeavour. See Chapter 3 for advice on making sound stock investment decisions.

A tremendous amount of data exists regarding stock market returns. In fact, in the U.S. markets, data going back more than two *centuries* document the fact that stocks have been a terrific long-term investment. The long-term returns from stocks that investors have enjoyed, and continue to enjoy, have been remarkably constant from one generation to the next.

Going all the way back to 1802, the U.S. stock market has produced an annual return of 8.3 percent, while inflation has grown at 1.4 percent per year. Thus, after subtracting for inflation, stocks have appreciated about 6.9 percent faster annually than the rate of inflation. The U.S. stock market returns have consistently and substantially beaten the rate of inflation over the years.

Stocks don't exist only in Canada and the United States, of course. More than a few investors seem to forget this fact, as they did during the sizzling performance of the Canadian and U.S. stock markets during the late 1990s. As discussed in the earlier section "Diversify for a gentler ride," one advantage of buying and holding overseas stocks is that they don't always move in tandem with North American stocks. As a result, overseas stocks help diversify your portfolio.

In addition to enabling Canadian investors to diversify, investing overseas has proved to be profitable. The investment banking firm Morgan Stanley tracks the performance of stocks in both economically established countries and so-called emerging economies. As the name suggests, countries with *emerging economies* (for example, Brazil, China, India, Malaysia, Mexico, Russia, and Taiwan) are "behind" economically, but show high rates of growth and progress.

Stocks are the best long-term performers, but they have more volatility than bonds and T-bills. A balanced portfolio gets you most of the long-term returns of stocks without much of the volatility.

Real estate returns

Over the years, real estate has proved to be about as lucrative as investing in the stock market. Whenever there's a real estate downturn, folks question this historic fact. However, just as stock prices have down periods, so, too, do real estate markets.

The fact that real estate offers solid long-term returns makes sense because growth in the economy, in jobs, and in population ultimately fuels the demand for real estate.

Consider what has happened to the Canadian population over the past two centuries. In 1867, a mere 3.5 million people lived within our borders. In 1900, that figure grew to over 5 million, and by 1929, it had doubled to over 10 million. At the time of writing, it's about 37 million. All these people need places to live, and as long as jobs exist, the income from jobs largely fuels the demand for housing.

Businesses and people have an understandable tendency to cluster in major cities and suburban towns. Although some people commute, most people and businesses locate near major highways, airports, and so on. Thus, real estate prices in and near major metropolises and suburbs generally appreciate the most. Consider the areas of the world that have the most expensive real estate prices: Hong Kong, Singapore, London, San Francisco, New York, and Boston. Here at home, our most expensive cities are Vancouver and Toronto. What these areas have in common are lots of businesses and people and limited land.

Contrast these areas with the many rural parts of Canada where the price of real estate is relatively low because of the abundant supply of buildable land and the relatively lower demand for housing.

Small business returns

You have several choices for tapping into the exciting potential of the small business world (see Chapter 7). If you have the drive and determination, you can start your own small business. Or perhaps you have what it takes to buy an existing small business. If you obtain the necessary capital and skills to assess opportunities and risk, you can invest in someone else's small business.

What potential returns can you get from small business? Small business owners who do something they really enjoy will tell you that the nonfinancial returns can be major. But the financial rewards can be attractive as well.

Every year, *Forbes* magazine publishes a list of the world's wealthiest individuals. Perusing this list shows that most of these people built their wealth by taking a significant ownership stake and starting a small business that became large. These individuals achieved extraordinarily high returns (often in excess of hundreds of percent per year) on the amounts they invested to get their companies off the ground.

You may also achieve potentially high returns from buying and improving an existing small business. Such small business investment returns may be a good deal lower than the returns you may gain from starting a business from scratch.

Unlike the stock market, where plenty of historic rate-of-return data exists, data on the success — or lack thereof — that investors have had with investing in small private companies is harder to come by. Smart venture capitalist firms operate a fun and lucrative business: They identify and invest money in smaller start-up companies that they hope will grow rapidly and eventually go public. Venture capitalists allow outsiders to invest with them via limited partnerships. To gain entry, you generally need $1 million to invest, although there are some exceptions from time to time. (No one ever said this was an equal-opportunity investment club!)

Venture capitalists, also known as *general partners,* typically skim off 20 percent of the profits and also charge limited partnership investors a hefty 2 percent to 3 percent annual fee on the amount that they've invested. The return that's left over for the limited partnership investors isn't always stupendous. According to Venture Economics, a U.S. firm that tracks limited partners' returns, venture funds have averaged comparable annual returns to what stock market investors have earned on average over this same period. The general partners that run venture capital funds make more than the limited partners do.

You can attempt to do what the general partners do in venture capital firms and invest directly in small private companies. But you're likely to be investing in much smaller and simpler companies. Earning venture capitalist returns isn't easy to do. If you think you're up to the challenge, you find out more about how to invest in small business in Chapter 7.

2

Getting Your Financial House in Order

Before you make any great, wealth-building investments, you need to get your financial house in order. Understanding and implementing some simple personal financial management concepts can pay off big for you in the decades ahead.

You want to know how to earn healthy returns on your investments without getting clobbered, right? Who doesn't? Although you generally must accept greater risk to have the potential for earning higher returns (see Chapter 1), this chapter tells you about some high-return, low-risk investments. You have a right to be skeptical about such investments, but don't stop reading this chapter yet. Here, you'll find some easy-to-tap opportunities for managing your money that you may have overlooked.

The Importance of Establishing an Emergency Reserve

You never know what life will bring, so having a readily accessible reserve of cash to meet unexpected expenses makes good financial sense. If you have a sister who works on Bay Street as an investment banker or a wealthy and understanding parent, you can use one of them as your emergency reserve. (Although you should ask them how they feel about that before you count on receiving funding from them.) If you don't have a wealthy family member, the ball's in your court to establish a reserve.

Make sure you have quick access to at least three months' to as much as six months' worth of living expenses. Keep this emergency money in a high-interest savings account or a Tax-Free Savings Account (TFSA). You may also be able to borrow against your home equity should you find yourself in a bind, but this option are much less desirable.

If you don't have a financial safety net, you may be forced into selling an investment that you've worked hard for. And selling some investments, such as real estate, costs big money (because of transaction costs, taxes, and so on).

Consider the case of Warren, who owned his home and rented an investment property on the west coast. He felt, and appeared to be, financially successful. But then Warren lost his job, accumulated sizable medical expenses, and had to sell his investment property to come up with cash for living expenses. Warren didn't have enough equity in his home to borrow. He didn't have other sources — a wealthy relative, for example — to borrow from either, so he was stuck selling his investment property. Warren wasn't able to purchase another investment property and missed out on the large appreciation the property earned over the subsequent two decades. Between the costs of selling and taxes, getting rid of the investment property cost Warren about 15 percent of its sales price. Ouch!

A Look at Your Debts

Yes, paying down debts is boring, but it makes your investment decisions less difficult. Rather than spending so much of your time investigating specific investments, paying off your debts (if you have them and your cash coming in exceeds the cash going out) may be your best high-return, low-risk investment. Consider the interest rate you pay and your investing alternatives to determine which debts you should pay off.

Consumer debt

Borrowing via credit cards, auto loans, and the like is an expensive way to borrow. Banks and other lenders charge higher interest rates for consumer debt than for debt for investments, such as real estate and business. The reason: Consumer loans are the riskiest type of loan for a lender.

Many folks have credit card or other consumer debt, such as an auto loan, that costs 8 percent, 10 percent, 12 percent, or perhaps as much as 18 percent per year in interest (some credit cards whack you with interest rates exceeding 20 percent if you make a late payment). Reducing and eventually eliminating this debt with your savings is like putting your money in an investment with a guaranteed *tax-free* return equal to the rate that you pay on your debt.

For example, if you have outstanding credit card debt at 15 percent interest, paying off that debt is the same as putting your money to work in an investment with a guaranteed 15 percent tax-free annual return. Because the interest on consumer debt isn't tax-deductible, you need to earn more than 15 percent by investing your money elsewhere in order to net 15 percent after paying taxes. Earning such high investing returns is highly unlikely, and in order to earn those returns, you'd be forced to take great risk.

Consumer debt is hazardous to your long-term financial health (not to mention damaging to your credit score and future ability to borrow for a home or other wise investments) because it encourages you to borrow against your future earnings. People often say such things as "I can't afford to buy most new cars for cash — look at how expensive they are!" That's true, new cars *are* expensive, so you need to set your sights lower and buy a good used car that you *can* afford. You can then invest the money you'd otherwise spend on your auto loan.

 However, using consumer debt may make sense if you're financing a business. If you don't have home equity, personal loans (through a credit card or auto loan) may actually be your lowest-cost source of small business financing.

Your mortgage

Paying off your mortgage more quickly is an "investment" for your spare cash that may make sense for your financial situation. However, the wisdom of making this financial move isn't as clear as paying off high-interest consumer debt because mortgage interest rates are generally lower. When used properly, debt can help you accomplish your goals — such as buying a home or starting a business — and make you money in the long run. Borrowing to buy a home generally makes sense. Over the long term, homes generally appreciate in value.

If your financial situation has changed or improved since you first needed to borrow mortgage money, you need to reconsider how much mortgage debt you need or want. Even if your income hasn't escalated or you haven't inherited vast wealth, your frugality may allow you to pay down some of your debt sooner than the lender requires. Whether paying down your debt sooner makes sense for you depends on a number of factors, including your other investment options and goals.

When evaluating whether to pay down your mortgage faster, you need to compare your mortgage interest rate with your investments' rates of return (see Chapter 1). Suppose you have a fixed-rate mortgage with an interest rate of 6 percent. If you decide to make investments instead of paying down your mortgage more quickly, your investments need to produce an average annual rate of return, of about 6 percent to come out ahead financially. If this money is being invested outside of a tax-deferred Registered Retirement Savings Plan (RRSP) or TFSA, you'll need to earn anywhere from 8 percent to 12 percent — depending on the type of investment — so that *after* taxes, you've earned 6 percent.

Besides the most common reason of lacking the money to do so, other good reasons *not* to pay off your mortgage any quicker than necessary include the following:

- **You contribute instead to your RRSP or other retirement plan, especially if your employer matches your contribution.** Paying off your mortgage faster has no tax benefit. By contrast, putting additional money into a retirement plan can immediately reduce your income tax burden. The more years you have until retirement, the greater the benefit you receive if you invest in your retirement plans. Thanks to the compounding of your retirement plan investments without the drain of taxes, you can actually earn a lower rate of return on your investments than you pay on your mortgage and still come out ahead. (See the later section "How to Fund Your Registered Retirement Savings Plan" for more information.)

- **You're willing to invest in growth-oriented, volatile investments, such as stocks and real estate.** In order to have a reasonable chance of earning more on your investments than it costs you to borrow on your mortgage, you must be aggressive with your investments. As discussed in Chapter 1, stocks and real estate have produced annual average rates of return of about 8 percent to 10 percent. You can earn even more by creating your own small business or by investing in others' businesses. Paying down a mortgage ties up more of your capital, reducing your ability to make other attractive investments. To more aggressive investors, paying off the house seems downright boring — the financial equivalent of watching paint dry.

Note: You have no guarantee of earning high returns from growth-type investments, which can easily drop 20 percent or more in value over a year or two.

- **Paying down the mortgage depletes your emergency reserves.** Psychologically, some people feel uncomfortable paying off debt more quickly if it diminishes their savings and investments. You probably don't want to pay down your debt if doing so depletes your financial safety cushion. Make sure that you have access — through a high-interest savings account, money market fund, or other sources (a family member, for example) — to at least three months' worth of living expenses (as explained in the earlier section "The Importance of Establishing an Emergency Reserve").

Don't be tripped up by the misconception that somehow a real estate market downturn, such as the one that most areas experienced in the mid- to late 2000s, will harm you more if you pay down your mortgage. Your home is worth what it's worth — its value has *nothing* to do with your debt load. Unless you're willing to walk away from your home and send the keys to the bank (also known as *default*), you suffer the full effect of a price decline, regardless of your mortgage size, if real estate prices drop.

How to Establish Your Financial Goals

You may have just one purpose for investing money, or you may desire to invest money for several different purposes simultaneously. Either way, you should establish your financial goals before you begin investing. Otherwise, you won't know how much to save.

For example, when one investor was in his twenties, he put away some money for retirement, but also saved a stash so he could hit the eject button from his job. He knew that he wanted to pursue an entrepreneurial path and that in the early years of starting his own business, he couldn't count on an income as stable or as large as the one he made from his job.

The investor invested his two "pots" of money — one for retirement and the other for his small business cushion — quite differently. As discussed in the later section "The Right Investment Mix," you can afford to take more risk with the money you plan on using longer term. So, he invested the bulk of his retirement nest egg in stock mutual funds.

With the money he saved for the start-up of his small business, he took an entirely different track. He had no desire to put this money in risky stocks — what if the market plummeted just as he was ready to leave the security of his full-time job? Thus, he kept this money safely invested in a money market fund that had a decent yield but didn't fluctuate in value.

Track your savings rate

To accomplish your financial goals (and some personal goals), you need to save money, and you also need to know your savings rate. Your *savings rate* is the percentage of your past year's income that you saved and didn't spend. Without even doing the calculations, you may already know that your rate of savings is low, nonexistent, or negative and that you need to save more.

Part of being a smart investor involves figuring out how much you need to save to reach your goals. Not knowing what you want to do a decade or more from now is perfectly normal — after all, your goals and needs evolve over the years. But that doesn't mean you should just throw your hands in the air and not make an effort to see where you stand today and think about where you want to be in the future.

An important benefit of knowing your savings rate is that you can better assess how much risk you need to take to accomplish your goals. Seeing the amount that you need to save to achieve your dreams may encourage you to take more risk with your investments.

During your working years, if you consistently save about 10 percent of your annual income, you're probably saving enough to meet your goals (unless you want to retire at a relatively young age). On average, most people need about 75 percent of their preretirement income throughout retirement to maintain their standards of living.

If you're one of the many people who don't save enough, you need to do some homework. To save more, you need to reduce your spending, increase your income, or both. For most people, reducing spending is the more feasible way to save.

To reduce your spending, first figure out where your money goes. You may have some general idea, but you need to have facts. Get out your chequebook register, examine your online bill-paying records, and review your credit card bills and any other documentation that shows your spending history. Tally up how much you spend on dining out, operating your car(s), paying your taxes, and everything else. After you have this information, you can begin to prioritize and make the necessary trade-offs to reduce your spending and increase your savings rate. Earning more income may help boost your savings rate as well. Perhaps you can get a higher-paying job or increase the number of hours that you work. But if you already work a lot, reining in your spending is usually better for your emotional and economic well-being.

If you don't know how to evaluate and reduce your spending or haven't thought about your retirement goals, looked into what you can expect from the Canada Pension Plan (CPP) or Quebec Pension Plan (QPP) and social security, or calculated how much you should save for retirement, now's the time to do so.

Determine your investment tastes

Many good investing choices exist: You can invest in real estate, the stock market, mutual funds, exchange-traded funds (ETFs), or your own or some else's small business. Or you can pay down mortgage debt more quickly. What makes sense for you depends on your goals, as well as your personal preferences. If you detest risk taking and volatile investments, paying down your mortgage, as recommended earlier in this chapter, may make more sense than investing in the stock market.

To determine your general investment tastes, think about how you would deal with an investment that plunges 20 percent, 40 percent, or more in a few years or less. Some aggressive investments can fall fast (see Chapter 1 for examples). You shouldn't go into the stock market, real estate, or the small business investment arena if such a drop is likely to cause you to sell low or make you a miserable, anxious wreck. If you haven't tried riskier investments yet, you may want to experiment a bit to see how you feel with your money invested in them.

A simple way to "mask" the risk of volatile investments is to *diversify* your portfolio — that is, to put your money into different investments. Not watching prices too closely helps, too — that's one of the reasons real estate investors are less likely to bail out when the market declines. Stock market investors, unfortunately, can get daily and even minute-by-minute price updates. Add that fact to the quick phone call or click of your computer mouse that it takes to dump a stock in a flash, and you have all the ingredients for shortsighted investing — and potential financial disaster.

How to Fund Your Registered Retirement Savings Plan

Saving money is difficult for most people. Don't make a tough job impossible by forsaking the tax benefits that come from contributing money to — and investing inside — an RRSP.

The basics of Registered Retirement Savings Plans

The only condition you have to meet to be able to contribute to an RRSP is you have to have what the government calls *earned income*. You work hard for any kind of dollars that flow into your household, but it doesn't all qualify. For most people, their *earned income* is their salary, along with any bonuses or commissions. If you're self-employed or an active partner in a business, it includes any net income from your business. Earned income also includes any taxable alimony and maintenance payments, as well as any research grants, royalties, and net rental income.

If you have any earned income in a year, you can contribute up to 18 percent of that total to your RRSP in the following year. That is only one of three limitations that put a ceiling on how much you can contribute. There is a straight dollar ceiling set, plus your maximum may be further reduced if you belong to a company pension plan. Here are the specific rules:

- Regardless of how much earned income you have, there is an absolute maximum dollar amount you can contribute for any one year. For 2019, the maximum RRSP contribution limit is $26,500.

- The maximum amount you're allowed to contribute may be further reduced if you belong to a company pension plan. The government calculates the value of contributions made to your employer-sponsored pension plan, called a pension adjustment, and deducts this from whichever is less — the absolute dollar maximum allowed for the year or 18 percent of your earned income — to arrive at your allowable contribution.

Your pension adjustment for a given year should appear in that year's T4 slip you receive from your employer. (It should also be stated on the Notice of Assessment you receive in the spring after you file your tax return for the previous year.)

Tax benefits

RRSPs should be called "tax-reduction accounts" — if they were, people might be more motivated to contribute to them. Contributions to these plans are tax deductible. Suppose you pay about 36 percent between federal and provincial income taxes on your last dollars of income (see the section "Tax brackets" later in this chapter). With an RRSP, you can save yourself about $360 in taxes for every $1,000 you contribute in the year that you make your contribution.

After your money is in a retirement plan, any interest, dividends, and appreciation grow inside the account without current taxation. You defer taxes on all the accumulating gains and profits until you withdraw your money down the road. In the meantime, more of your money works for you over a long period of time.

Deductions and contributions

It pays to understand the language around RRSPs, which can be confusing. Not understanding the basics can leave you missing out on some of their benefits.

The key danger comes from the use of two terms. The first is *contribution limit*. You might assume this refers to just how much money you can put into your RRSP in any one year. Not so. The second term is similar, *deduction limit*. Again, you might understandably think this refers to how much of your RRSP deduction you can claim in any one year. Wrong again.

In both cases, what is actually being addressed is how much your earned income in any one year gives you in terms of a dollar amount you can contribute to your RRSP. But you aren't required to contribute that money in that same year. Plus, in prior years, you may not have put in the maximum for each individual year. These unused sums — often called *contribution room* — are carried forward and can be both contributed to your RRSP and deducted from your income in future years. As a result, the amount you contribute to your RRSP and subsequently claim as a deduction on your tax return can be far in excess of your contribution limit or allowable deduction for that same year.

Say that based on your last year's salary, your new allowable contribution is $5,000, but you only contribute $2,000. Next year, your new allowable contribution is another $5,000, based on your income this year. This means the amount you can put into your RRSP will then be the sum of $5,000 and the $3,000 of allowable contribution you didn't use this year, for a total of $8,000.

When it comes to your RRSP contribution, it's not a case of "use it or lose it." If you don't put in the full amount you're allowed to in any given year, you can carry forward that amount — your *RRSP deduction limit* — and use it in the future. Think of it as having an ongoing allowable contribution account. Any time you have earned income, the next year you can add to your allowable contribution account the difference between the amount that year's earned income gave you the right to contribute and what you actually put into your RRSP.

An early start for maximum profits

Failing to take full advantage of registered retirement plans early in their working lives is one of the single most common mistakes investors make when it comes to RRSPs and Registered Pension Plans (RPPs). Often this is because of their enthusiasm to spend or invest outside of registered retirement plans. Not investing inside tax-sheltered retirement plans can cost you hundreds, perhaps thousands, of dollars per year in lost tax savings. Add that loss up over the many years that you work and save, and not taking advantage of an RRSP or RPP can easily cost you tens of thousands to hundreds of thousands of dollars in the long term. Ouch!

To take advantage of registered retirement plans and the tax savings that accompany them, you must first spend less than you earn. Only after you spend less than you earn can you afford to contribute to a registered retirement plan (unless you already happen to have a stash of cash from previous savings or inheritance).

If you enjoy spending money and living for today, you should be more motivated to start saving sooner. The longer you wait to save, the more you ultimately need to save and, therefore, the less you can spend today.

The sooner you start to save, the easier it will be to save enough to reach your goals because your contributions have more years to compound. Each decade you delay saving approximately doubles the percentage of your earnings that you need to save to meet your goals. For example, if saving 5 percent per year in your early 20s gets you to your retirement goal, waiting until your 30s to start may mean socking away 10 percent to reach that same goal; waiting until your 40s, 20 percent. Beyond that, the numbers get truly daunting.

How to Tame Your Taxes in Non-Retirement Accounts

When you invest outside of tax-deferred retirement plans, the profits and distributions on your money are subject to taxation. So, the non-retirement investments that make sense for you depend (at least partly) on your tax situation.

If you have money to invest, or if you're considering selling current investments that you hold, taxes should factor into your decision. But tax considerations alone shouldn't dictate how and where you invest your money. You should also weigh investment choices, your desire and the necessity to take risk, personal likes and dislikes, and the number of years you plan to hold the investment (see the later section "The Right Investment Mix" for more information on these other factors).

Tax brackets

You may not know it, but the government charges different tax rates for different parts of your annual income. You pay less tax on the *first* dollars of your earnings and more tax on the *last* dollars of your earnings. For example, if you were single and your taxable income totaled $50,000 during 2018, you paid no tax on the first $11,809. Depending on where you lived, you then paid — very approximately — combined federal and provincial taxes at the rate of 15 percent on the income between $11,810 and $20,000; 25 percent on your income between $20,000 and $47,000; and, finally, 32 percent on the income above $47,000 up to $50,000.

The reason this says *very approximately* is that you're taxed twice, even though you see only one income tax deduction on your pay statement:

- **You're taxed by the federal government on your taxable income.** The federal government has five marginal tax brackets, or tax rates.

- **You're taxed on the same taxable income by your province or territory.** Not only does each province or territory have its own particular tax brackets, but they don't correspond with those at the federal level. What makes matters even more complicated is that they also have many more tax levels — some as many as a dozen or more.

Your *marginal tax rate* is the rate of tax you pay on your *last,* or so-called *highest,* dollars of income. In the earlier example of a single person with taxable income of $50,000, that person's marginal tax rate is 32 percent. In other words, he effectively pays a 32 percent combined federal and provincial tax on his last dollars of income — those dollars earned between $47,000 and $50,000.

Knowing your marginal tax rate allows you to quickly calculate the following:

- Any additional taxes that you would pay on additional income

- The amount of taxes that you save if you contribute more money into retirement plans or reduce your taxable income (for example, if you choose investments that produce tax-free income)

 To find out more about tax rates, visit `www. canada.ca/en/revenue-agency/services/ tax/individuals/frequently-asked-questions- individuals/canadian-income-tax-rates- individuals-current-previous-years.html`.

What's taxed and when to worry

Interest you receive from bank accounts, Guaranteed Investment Certificates (GICs), and bonds is generally taxable. It's treated just like your regular income and taxed at the same rate. (Chapter 4 discusses bonds.)

If you sell stocks, bonds, rental property, or a position in a small business for more than what you paid, the profit is called a *capital gain.* Taxation on your *capital gains,* which is the *profit* (sales minus associated costs) on an investment, works under a unique system. You have to include half of your net gain in your income, which is then taxed at your marginal tax rate. The result is that the tax rate you effectively pay on capital gains — your *effective* tax rate — will be half of your marginal tax rate.

Suppose that you're in a marginal tax bracket of approximately 24 percent (note that exact tax rates and marginal tax brackets vary from province to province). Your effective tax rate on capital gains will be 12 percent. If you're in the next tax bracket, where your salary is taxed at 36 percent, your effective tax rate on capital gains is 18 percent, while those in the 42 percent marginal tax bracket will have an effective capital gains tax rate of 21 percent. Finally, those in the top 46 percent marginal tax bracket will have capital gains taxed at 23 percent.

Find out more information about capital gains here: www.canada.ca/en/revenue-agency/ services/tax/individuals/topics/about- your-tax-return/tax-return/completing-a- tax-return/personal-income/line- 127-capital-gains/calculating-reporting- your-capital-gains-losses.html.

Any *eligible dividends* you receive from Canadian corporations are taxed at the lowest effective rate. (Dividends from foreign corporations are treated and taxed just like your regular income.) A rather strange formula is used to determine the tax rate on Canadian dividends. This is because dividends are the distribution of a company's after-tax profits, so you receive a special tax credit to prevent the same profits from being taxed twice.

First, the amount of the dividend actually received is increased — *grossed up* — to reflect what the corporation is assumed to have made pretax. The gross-up percentage is regularly adjusted. This inflated number is what you show on your tax return as the amount of your dividend income. To offset this amount, you then get a federal dividend tax credit. Combined with a provincial tax credit, this means the top tax rate on dividends from public Canadian companies, depending on the province, will be approximately 30 percent to 40 percent. The levels of the provincial tax credits for dividends range widely, as do the levels of income at which they apply. That said, in most provinces you can receive just shy of $40,000 in income from eligible dividends before you have to pay any tax on that income.

For more about eligible dividends, visit www.canada.ca/en/revenue-agency/services/tax/individuals/topics/about-your-tax-return/tax-return/completing-a-tax-return/personal-income/line-120-taxable-amount-dividends-eligible-other-than-eligible-taxable-canadian-corporations.html.

The lower your overall income level, the lower the tax rate for any dividends you receive. But there's more: In most provinces, if your income is below certain levels, not only is your dividend income not taxed, but the tax you owe on income from other sources, including your regular job, is reduced. How? For lower-income earners, the marginal tax rate for eligible dividends is actually negative. (The lowest dividend

rate? In Ontario in 2018, if your taxable income was between $15,087 and $19,819, the rate was *negative* 13.69 percent.) When there is a negative marginal tax rate for dividends, the dividend tax credit you earn not only offsets any tax due on the dividend income, but also reduces tax payable on other income. If your marginal tax rate for dividends is –10 percent, for example, a dollar of dividend income would mean you'd pay $0.10 less overall in taxes than you would without the dollar of dividend income.

Use these strategies to reduce the taxes you pay on investments that are exposed to taxation:

- **Invest in tax-friendly stock funds.** Mutual funds that tend to trade less tend to produce lower capital gains distributions. For mutual funds held outside tax-sheltered registered retirement plans, this reduced trading effectively increases an investor's total rate of return.

Index funds are mutual funds that invest in a relatively static portfolio of securities, such as stocks and bonds (this is also true of some ETFs). They don't attempt to beat the market. Instead, they invest in the securities to mirror or match the performance of an underlying index, such as the S&P/TSX Composite Index or the Standard & Poor's 500 (see Chapter 3). Although index funds can't beat the market, the typical actively managed fund doesn't either, and index funds have several advantages over actively managed funds.

See Chapter 5 to find out more about tax-friendly stock mutual funds, which includes some non-index funds, and ETFs.

- **Invest in tax-friendly stocks.** Companies that pay little in the way of dividends reinvest more of their profits back into the company. If you invest outside of a retirement plan, unless you need income to live on, minimize your exposure to stocks with dividends. Be aware that low-dividend stocks tend to be more volatile.

- **Invest in small business and real estate.** The growth in value of business and real estate assets isn't taxed until you sell the asset. However, the current income that small business and real estate assets produce is taxed as ordinary income.

The Right Investment Mix

Diversifying your investments helps buffer your portfolio from being sunk by one or two poor performers. This section explains how to mix up a great recipe of investments.

Consider your age

When you're younger and you have more years until you plan to use your money, you should keep larger amounts of your long-term investment money in *growth* (ownership) vehicles, such as stocks, real estate, and small business. As discussed in Chapter 1, the attraction of these types of investments is the potential to really grow your money. The risk: The value of your portfolio can fall from time to time.

The younger you are, the more time your investments have to recover from a bad fall. In this respect, investments are a bit like people. If a 30-year-old and an 80-year-old both fall on a concrete sidewalk, odds are higher that the younger person will fully recover and the older person may not. Such falls sometimes disable older people.

 A long-held guiding principle says to subtract your age from 110 and invest the resulting number as a percentage of money to place in growth (ownership) investments. So, if you're 35 years old,

110 − 35 = 75 percent of your investment money can be in growth investments. If you want to be more aggressive, subtract your age from 120: 120 − 35 = 85 percent of your investment money can be in growth investments.

Note that even retired people should still have a healthy chunk of their investment dollars in growth vehicles like stocks. A 70-year-old person may want to totally avoid risk, but doing so is generally a mistake. Such a person can live another two or three decades. If you live longer than anticipated, you can run out of money if it doesn't continue to grow.

These tips are only general guidelines and apply to money that you invest for the long term (ideally for ten years or more). For money that you need to use in the shorter term, such as within the next several years, more aggressive growth investments aren't appropriate. See Chapters 4 and 5 for short-term investment ideas.

Make the most of your investment options

No hard-and-fast rules dictate how to allocate the percentage that you've earmarked for growth among specific investments like stocks and real estate. Part of how you decide to allocate your investments depends on the types of investments that you want to focus on. Diversifying in stocks worldwide can be prudent as well as profitable.

Here are some general guidelines to keep in mind:

- **Take advantage of your registered retirement plans.** Unless you need accessible money for shorter-term non-retirement goals, why pass up the free extra returns from the tax benefits of an RRSP or RPP (a company or corporate plan)?

- **Take advantage of a TFSA.** The capital gains, dividends, and interest you earn on money inside these accounts are tax-free, as are any withdrawals. Put short-term money such as your emergency funds into a TFSA. Also consider sheltering savings in a TFSA if you're already contributing the maximum to your RRSP.

- **Don't pile your money into investments that gain lots of attention.** Many investors make this mistake, especially those who lack a thought-out plan to buy stocks. Chapter 3 provides numerous illustrations of the perils of buying attention-grabbing stocks.

- **Have the courage to be a contrarian.** No one likes to feel that he's jumping aboard a sinking ship or supporting a losing cause. However, just like shopping for something at retail stores, the best time to buy something of quality is when its price is reduced.

- **Diversify.** As discussed in Chapter 1, the values of different investments don't move in tandem. So, when you invest in growth investments, such as stocks or real estate, your portfolio's value will have a smoother ride if you diversify properly.

- **Invest more in what you know.** Over the years, there have been successful investors who have built substantial wealth without spending gobs of their free time researching, selecting, and monitoring investments. Some investors, for example, concentrate more on real estate because that's what they best understand and feel comfortable with. Others put more money in stocks for the same reason. No one-size-fits-all code exists for successful investors. Just be careful that you don't put all your investing eggs in the same basket (for example, don't load up on stocks in the same industry that you believe you know a lot about).

- **Don't invest in too many different things.** Diversification is good to a point. If you purchase so many investments that you can't perform a basic annual review of all of them (for example, reading the annual report from your mutual fund), you have too many investments.

- **Be more aggressive with investments inside retirement plans.** When you hit your retirement years, you'll probably begin to live off your non-retirement plan investments first. Allowing your retirement accounts to continue growing can generally defer your tax dollars.

Therefore, you should be relatively less aggressive with investments outside of retirement plans because that money may be invested for a shorter time period.

How to Invest for University or College

There's no doubt that having kids is one of the — if not *the* — most expensive decisions you'll ever make. From paying for diapers to having to buy a heck of a lot more groceries when your kids become teenagers, having children is a costly affair. But it can feel downright punitive when you start thinking about what it will cost to get them a postsecondary education.

That's not exactly welcome news for those already trying to pay off their mortgages and save for retirement. What can you do? Surprisingly, one of the best tactics is often to focus only on your first two goals and ignore the third. If you work hard and knock down your mortgage, you'll have a good chance of being able to reduce or even eliminate your mortgage payments by the time the little ones are ready to go to university. If you've knocked a good deal off of your mortgage, you'll also be in the position to borrow against the equity you've built up in your home to pay for educational expenses.

By working hard to grow your RRSP, hopefully you'll accumulate a good-sized sum that has built up some compounding steam. If you're accustomed to "paying yourself first" — regularly diverting a portion of your income to your RRSP — you can turn your financial sights away from your old age and toward your children's educational bills while they're at school, and resume your RRSP contributions after they graduate.

Some folks may not feel comfortable unless they're putting away some dollars specifically earmarked for education. Others may be in the enviable position of being able to set aside savings for future educational costs while also taking care of their mortgages and building up their RRSPs. If you want to start an education savings program, you have two basic ways to do it, each with some distinct benefits and drawbacks you need to consider. The approach that works best for you will be determined by your family circumstances, your outlook, and your sense of where your children are heading.

Make the most out of a Registered Education Savings Plan

If you've got a basic understanding of how RRSPs work, then you're already halfway to making sense of Registered Education Savings Plans (RESPs). However, there are also some key differences to be aware of. Much like an RRSP, an RESP lets you set money aside and defer tax on the gains you make on that money while it's inside the plan. When you put money into an RRSP, you also get a tax deduction for your contribution. In contrast, you don't get to deduct money you put into an RESP from your income when figuring out your tax bill for the year.

And, as with your RRSP, when you withdraw money from an RESP, it's treated as income and taxed accordingly. But the big difference is that it's treated as income for your child. Given that their other income — if they have any — will be low, the amount of tax they'll have to pay will be negligible or nonexistent.

You can set up an RESP for each of your children, with a lifetime maximum contribution ceiling of $50,000. When RESPs were first introduced, there was also an annual limit on how much you could contribute, but that has been eliminated.

What makes RESPs financially friendly is that the government tops up your contributions. Under the Canada Education Savings Grant (CESG), the federal government will put in another 20 percent of any contribution you make, to a maximum of $500 per year. The grant is available every year the beneficiary of the RESP is under the age of 18, up to a maximum of $7,200. (The grant amounts aren't included when calculating your contribution limits.)

If you don't make the most use of the CESG in any one year by contributing $2,500 and receiving the maximum annual grant of $500, don't worry. If you put in less in any one year, you can earn the untapped grant in future years. However, in any one single year, the CESG per beneficiary is limited to the lesser of $1,000 or 20 percent of the unused CESG room.

Like RRSPs, you can invest money inside an RESP in a wide choice of investments, including the many types of mutual funds and even individual stocks. (Be sure to opt for a self-directed RESP, not one of the group plans that have higher fees and more restrictions.) If you have more than one child, you can set up a family plan that makes it simpler and easier — you can use a single RESP for all your children.

If your child does not pursue a further education that allows him or her to use the money inside the plan, you can take out the original contributions without any penalty. However, you'll have to return any grants you've received under the CESG. In addition, the money you've made on any grants, as well as on your own contributions, may be taxable.

If the beneficiary is not a postsecondary student by age 21 and the plan has been running for at least ten years, you can transfer up to $50,000 of the plan's profits to your own or your spouse's RRSP. However, you must have sufficient unused RRSP contribution room available. (The result is that the RRSP deduction you receive will offset any taxes including the RESP's earnings in your income). Any of the plan's profits that don't get sheltered in this way are taxed at your full marginal tax rate. In addition, you pay an extra 20 percent penalty. On top of your tax bill, that could mean giving up as much as 65 percent of the profits. Ouch!

Allocate university investments

If you keep up to 80 percent of your university investment money in stocks (diversified worldwide) with the remainder in bonds when your child is young, you can maximize the money's growth potential without taking extraordinary risk. As your child makes his or her way through the later years of elementary school, you need to begin to make the mix more conservative — scale back the stock percentage to 50 percent or 60 percent. Finally, in the years just before your child enters college, whittle the stock portion down to no more than 20 percent or so.

Diversified mutual funds (which invest in stocks in Canada and internationally) and bonds are ideal vehicles to use when you invest for college. Be sure to choose funds that fit your tax situation if you invest your funds in non-retirement plans. See Chapter 5 for more information.

3

Building Wealth
with Stocks

Some people liken investing in the stock market to gambling. A real casino structures its games — such as slot machines, blackjack, and roulette — so that, in aggregate, the casino owners siphon off a major chunk (40 percent) of the money that people gamble with. The vast majority of casino patrons lose money — in some cases, all of it. The few who leave with more money than they came with are usually people who are lucky and are smart enough to quit while they're ahead.

Fortunately, the stock market isn't a casino — far from it. Shares of stock, which represent portions of ownership in companies, offer a way for people of modest and wealthy means, and everybody in between, to invest in companies and build wealth. History shows that long-term investors can win in the stock market because it appreciates over the years. That said, some people who remain active in the market over many years manage to lose some money because of easily avoidable mistakes, which this chapter can keep you from making.

How You Make Money in Stocks

 When you purchase a share of a company's stock, you can profit from your ownership in two ways:

- **Dividends:** Many stocks pay dividends. Companies generally make some profits during the year. Some high-growth companies reinvest most or all their profits right back into the business. Many companies, however, pay out some of their profits to shareholders in the form of quarterly *dividends.*

- **Appreciation:** When the price per share of your stock rises to a level greater than you originally paid for it, you make money. This profit, however, is only on paper until you sell the stock, at which time you realize a *capital gain.* Of course, the stock price per share can fall below what you originally paid as well (in which case you have a loss on paper unless you realize that loss by selling).

If you add together dividends and appreciation, you arrive at your total return. Stocks differ in the dimensions of these possible returns, particularly with respect to dividends.

The Definition of "the Market"

You invest in stocks to share in the rewards of capitalistic economies. When you invest in stocks, you do so through the stock market. What is the stock market? Everybody talks about "the market" the same way they do the largest city nearby ("the city"):

The market is down 137 points today.

With the market hitting new highs, isn't now a bad time to invest?

The market seems ready for a fall.

In general, when people talk about "the market," they're usually referring to the Canadian stock market. More specifically, they're usually talking about the performance of the S&P/TSX Composite Index. The S&P/TSX Composite tracks the performance of larger-company Canadian stocks. In general, the index is made up of the companies with the largest *market capitalization* — their stock price multiplied by the number of shares outstanding. To be included in the index, companies must meet a number of other criteria. The most important is liquidity, which is measure by looking at the number of shares traded, the number of transactions, and the total value.

The S&P/TSX Composite Index includes a broad, representative basket of Canadian companies that are mainstays of the economy. This includes all the big banks; insurance behemoths Great-West Lifeco and Sun Life; mining majors Barrick Gold, Franco-Nevada, and Teck Resources; plane, train, seadoo/skidoo maker Bombardier; engineering and construction conglomerate SNC-Lavalin; movie chain Cineplex; financiers Power Financial; oil and gas giants Imperial Oil, Enbridge, and Encana; tech mainstays BlackBerry, Descartes Systems, and Mitel Networks; retailers Hudson's Bay, Canadian Tire, and Sleep Country; real estate investors Granite and RioCan; communication kings Rogers and Shaw; and grocery chains Weston and Loblaw.

The index used to be called the TSE 300, but that came to an end in 2002. That year, all the indexes were revamped by Standard & Poor's, which also took over their administration. The number of companies included can now vary depending on how many meet the requirements. Recently, the number has been running about 250.

In the United States, of course, "the market" refers to the U.S. stock market. And there the most widely watched stock market scoreboard is the Dow Jones Industrial Average.

This index was created by Charles Dow and Eddie Jones. Dow and Jones were two reporters who, in their 30s, started publishing a paper that you may have heard of — *The Wall Street Journal* — in 1889. Like the modern-day version, the 19th-century *Wall Street Journal* reported current financial news. Dow and Jones also compiled stock prices of larger, important companies and created and calculated indexes to track the performance of the U.S. stock market.

The Dow Jones Industrial Average ("the Dow") market index tracks the performance of 30 large companies that are headquartered in the United States. The Dow 30 includes companies such as telecommunications giant Verizon Communications; airplane manufacturer Boeing; beverage maker Coca-Cola; oil giant Exxon Mobil; technology behemoths Apple, IBM, Intel, and Microsoft; drugmakers Merck and Pfizer; fast-food king McDonald's; and retailers Home Depot and Walmart.

Some people criticize the Dow index for encompassing so few companies and for a lack of diversity. The 30 stocks that make up the Dow aren't the 30 largest or the 30 best companies in the United States. They just so happen to be the 30 companies that senior staff members at the *Wall Street Journal* think reflect the diversity of the economy in the United States (although utility and transportation stocks are excluded and tracked in other Dow indexes). The 30 stocks in the Dow change over time as companies merge, decline, and rise in importance. For example, General Electric (GE) was the last original member of the Dow Jones Industrial Average before being replaced by Walgreens in June 2018.

Major stock market indexes

Just as New York City isn't the only city to visit or live in, the 30 stocks in the Dow Jones Industrial Average are far from representative of all the different types of stocks that you can invest in. Here are some other important market indexes and the types of stocks they track:

- **Standard & Poor's (S&P) 500:** Like the Dow Jones Industrial Average, the S&P 500 tracks the price of 500 larger-company U.S. stocks. These 500 big companies account for more than 70 percent of the total market value of the tens of thousands of stocks traded in the United States. So, the S&P 500 is a much broader and more representative index of the larger-company stocks in the United States than the Dow Jones Industrial Average is.

  Unlike the Dow index, which is primarily calculated by adding the current share price of each of its component stocks, the S&P 500 index is calculated by adding the total market value (capitalization) of its component stocks.

- **S&P/TSX 60:** This index represents the leading large-cap Canadian companies in leading industries. To be considered for the index, a company must be part of the S&P/TSX Composite Index, but those with poor liquidity don't make the grade. An index committee chooses 60 of the largest companies that offer a representation of the major industries.

There's also a capped version of this index, which limits the weighting of any one stock to a maximum of 10 percent of the total market capitalization of all the stocks in the index. This was done to prevent situations where one company whose stock has soared and flopped (as Nortel's did in the late 1990s) dominates the index and gives an unbalanced reading of the market's overall performance. The S&P/TSX 60 Index is also the Canadian component of Standard & Poor's flagship S&P Global 1200 Index.

- **S&P/TSX Venture Composite Index:** This index is a broad measure of the performance of the TSX Venture Exchange, home to Canada's smaller and often much more speculative companies.

The index has a somewhat confusing past. When the Vancouver Stock Exchange and the Alberta Stock Exchange merged, the two exchanges were replaced by the new Canadian Venture Exchange (CDNX), and a new index — the Canadian Venture Exchange Index — was created. But that index was short-lived and was replaced by the new S&P/TSX Venture Composite Index in 2001. However, the new Venture index isn't a continuation of the old Canadian Venture Exchange index, but an entirely new index based on different rules and requirements. The Canadian Venture Exchange index was simply closed down, and the new index began on a different — and completely unconnected — level than its predecessor. The new index looks at market capitalization when determining eligibility, and the number of companies it includes is typically in the low 500 range.

- **Russell 2000:** This index tracks the market value of 2,000 smaller U.S. company stocks of various industries. Although small-company stocks tend to move in tandem with larger-company stocks over the longer term, it's not unusual for one to rise or fall more than the other or for one index to fall while the other rises in a given year. For example, in 2001, the Russell 2000 actually rose 2.5 percent while the S&P 500 fell 11.9 percent. In 2007, the Russell 2000 lost 1.6 percent versus a gain of 5.5 percent for the S&P 500.

Be aware that smaller-company stocks tend to be more volatile. (Chapter 1 discusses risks and returns in more detail.)

- **Wilshire 5000:** While the Wilshire 5000 index did contain just that number of companies when it was created in 1974, today it actually tracks the prices of around 3,500. Still, that number, and the fact that it includes stocks of U.S. companies of all sizes — small, medium, and large — means many consider this index the broadest and most representative of the overall U.S. stock market.

- **MSCI EAFE:** Stocks don't exist only in North America. MSCI's EAFE index tracks the prices of stocks in the other major developed countries of the world. *EAFE* stands for Europe, Australasia, and Far East.

- **MSCI Emerging Markets:** This index follows the value of stocks in the less economically developed but "emerging" countries, such as Brazil, China, Russia, Taiwan, India, South Africa, Chile, Mexico, and so on. These stock markets tend to be more volatile than those in established economies. During good economic times, emerging markets usually reward investors with higher returns, but stocks can fall farther and faster than stocks in developed markets.

Conspicuously absent from this list of major stock market indexes is the Nasdaq index. With the boom in technology stock prices in the late 1990s, CNBC and other financial media started broadcasting movements in the technology-laden Nasdaq index, thereby increasing investor interest and the frenzy surrounding technology stocks. Sector- (industry-) specific investing undermines diversification and places you in the role of a professional money manager in having to determine when and how much to invest in specific industry groups. You can largely ignore the Nasdaq, as well as other industry-concentrated indexes.

Reasons to use indexes

Indexes serve several purposes. First, they can quickly give you an idea of how particular types of stocks perform in comparison with other types of stocks. In 1998, for example, the S&P 500 was up 28.6 percent, whereas the small-company Russell 2000 index was down 2.5 percent. That same year, the MSCI foreign stock EAFE index rose 20.3 percent. In 2001, by contrast, the S&P 500 fell 11.9 percent, and the EAFE foreign stock index had an even worse year, falling 21.4 percent. In 2013, the S&P 500 surged 29.7 percent, while the foreign EAFE index returned 18 percent.

Indexes also allow you to compare or benchmark the performance of your stock market investments. If you invest primarily in large-company Canadian stocks, for example, you should compare the overall return of the stocks in your portfolio to a comparable index — in this case, the S&P/TSX Composite. (As discussed in Chapter 5, index mutual funds, which invest to match a major stock market index, offer a cost-effective, proven way to build wealth by investing in stocks.)

You may also hear about some other types of more narrowly focused indexes, including those that track the performance of stocks in particular industries, such as advertising, banking, computers, pharmaceuticals, restaurants, semiconductors, textiles, and utilities. Other indexes cover the stock markets of other countries, such as the United States, the United Kingdom, Japan, Shanghai, Germany, France, and Hong Kong.

Focusing your investments in the stocks of just one or two industries or smaller countries is dangerous due to the lack of diversification and your lack of expertise in making the difficult decision about what to invest in and when. So, you should ignore the narrower of these indexes. Many companies, largely out of desire for publicity, develop their own indexes. If the news media report on these indexes, the index developer obtains free advertising. (Chapter 5 discusses investing strategies, such as those that focus on value stocks or growth stocks, which also have market indexes.)

Stock-Buying Methods

When you invest in stocks, many (perhaps too many) choices exist. Besides the tens of thousands of stocks from which you can select, you also can invest in mutual funds, exchange-traded funds (ETFs), or hedge funds, or you can have an investment advisor select them for you.

Mutual funds and exchange-traded funds

If you're busy and suffer no delusions about your expertise, you'll love the best stock mutual funds and ETFs. Investing in stocks through these funds can be as simple as dialing a toll-free number or logging on to a fund company's website, completing some application forms, and zapping them some money.

Mutual funds take money invested by people like you and your neighbours and pool it in a single investment portfolio in securities, such as stocks and bonds. The portfolio is then professionally managed. Stock mutual funds, as the name suggests, invest primarily or exclusively in stocks (some stock funds sometimes invest a bit in other stuff, such as bonds).

ETFs are in many ways similar to mutual funds, specifically index funds (see Chapter 5), except that they trade on a stock exchange. One potential attraction is that some ETFs offer investors the potential for even lower operating expenses than comparable mutual funds and may be tax-friendlier. Chapter 5 expands on ETFs and explains which ones to consider.

Stock funds have many advantages:

- **Diversification:** Buying individual stocks on your own is relatively costly unless you buy reasonable chunks (100 shares or so) of each stock. But to buy 100 shares each in, say, a dozen companies' stocks to ensure diversification, you need about $60,000 if the stocks that you buy average $50 per share.

- **Professional management:** Even if you have big bucks to invest, funds offer something that you can't deliver: professional, full-time management. Fund managers peruse a company's financial statements and otherwise track and analyze its business strategy and market position. The best managers put in long hours and have lots of expertise and experience in the field. (If you've been misled into believing that with minimal effort you can rack up market-beating returns by selecting your own stocks, be sure to read the rest of this chapter.)

  Look at it this way: Funds are a huge time-saver. On your next day off, would you rather sit in front of your computer and do some research on semiconductor and toilet paper manufacturers, or would you rather enjoy dinner and a movie with family and friends?

- **Low costs — if you pick 'em right:** To convince you that funds aren't a good way for you to invest, those with a vested interest, such as stock-picking newsletter pundits, may point out the high fees that some funds charge. An element of truth rings here: Some funds are expensive, charging you 2 percent or 3 percent or more per year in operating expenses on top of hefty sales commissions.

But just as you wouldn't want to invest in a fund that a novice with no track record manages, why would you want to invest in a high-cost fund? Contrary to the "You get what you pay for" notion often trumpeted by those trying to sell you something at an inflated price, some of the best managers are the cheapest to hire. Through a *no-load* (commission-free) mutual fund, you can hire a professional, full-time money manager to invest $10,000 for a mere $50 to $150 per year. Some index funds and ETFs charge significantly less.

As with all investments, funds have some drawbacks. Consider the following:

- **The issue of control is a problem for some investors.** If you like being in control, sending your investment dollars to a seemingly black-box process where others decide when and in what to invest your money may unnerve you. However, you need to be more concerned about the potential blunders that you may make investing in individual stocks of your own choosing or, even worse, those stocks pitched to you by an investment advisor.

- **Taxes are a concern when you invest in funds outside of registered retirement plans.** Because the fund manager decides when to sell specific stock holdings, some funds may produce relatively high levels of taxable distributions. Fear not — simply select tax-friendly funds if taxes concern you.

Chapter 5 discusses investing in the best mutual funds and ETFs that offer a high-quality, time-efficient, and cost-efficient way to invest in stocks worldwide.

Hedge funds

Like mutual funds, *hedge funds* are a managed investment vehicle. In other words, an investment management team researches and manages the funds' portfolio. However, hedge funds are oriented to affluent investors and typically charge steep fees — a 1 percent to 1.5 percent annual management fee plus a 20 percent cut of the annual fund returns.

No proof exists that hedge funds as a group perform better than mutual funds. In fact, objective studies show inferior hedge fund returns, which makes sense. Those high hedge fund fees depress their returns. Notwithstanding the small number of hedge funds that have produced better long-term returns, too many affluent folks invest in hedge funds due to the funds' hyped marketing and the badge of exclusivity they offer.

Individual stocks

More than a few investing books suggest and enthusiastically encourage people to do their own stock picking. However, the vast majority of investors are better off *not* picking their own stocks.

You should educate yourself and take responsibility for your own financial affairs, but taking responsibility for your finances doesn't mean you should do *everything* yourself. Table 3-1 includes some things to consider about choosing your own stocks.

Good Reasons to Pick Your Own Stocks	Bad Reasons to Pick Your Own Stocks
You enjoy the challenge.	You think you can beat the best money managers. (If you can, you're in the wrong profession.)
You want to learn more about business.	You want more control over your investments, which you think may happen if you understand the companies that you invest in.
You have a substantial amount of money to invest.	You think that mutual funds are for people who aren't smart enough to choose their own stocks.
You're a buy-and-hold investor.	You're attracted to the ability to trade your stocks anytime you want.

Table 3-1: *The Pros and Cons of Buying Your Own Stocks*

Some popular investing books try to convince investors that they can do a better job than the professionals at picking their own stocks. Amateur investors, however, need to devote a lot of study to become proficient at stock selection. Many professional investors work up to 60 to 80 hours a week at investing, but you're unlikely to be willing to spend that much time on it. Don't let the popularity of those do-it-yourself stock-picking books lead you astray.

Choosing a stock isn't as simple as visiting a restaurant chain (or buying a pair of shoes or the latest gadget), liking it, buying its stock, and then sitting back and getting rich while watching your stock zoom to the moon.

If you invest in stocks, you know by now that guarantees don't exist. But as in many of life's endeavours, you can buy individual stocks in good and not-so-good ways. So, if you want to select your own individual stocks, check out the later section "How to Get Ready to Invest in Stocks."

SpotTimes to Buy and Sell with the Price-to-Earnings Ratio

After you know about the different types of stock markets and ways to invest in stocks, you may wonder how you can build wealth with stocks and not lose your shirt. Nobody wants to buy stocks before a big drop.

The stock market is reasonably efficient. A company's stock price normally reflects many smart people's assessments as to what is a fair price. So, it's not realistic for an investor to expect to discover a system for how to "buy low and sell high." Some professional investors may be able to spot good times to buy and sell particular stocks, but consistently doing so is enormously difficult.

The simplest and best way to make money in the stock market is to consistently and regularly feed new money into building a diversified and larger portfolio. If the market drops, you can use your new investment dollars to buy more shares. The danger of trying to time the market is that you may be "out" of the market when it appreciates greatly and "in" the market when it plummets.

Suppose you find out that the stock for Liz's Distinctive Jewellery sells for $50 per share and that another stock in the same industry, The Jazzy Jeweller, sells for $100. Which would you rather buy?

If you answer, "I don't have a clue because you didn't give me enough information," go to the head of the class. On its own, the price per share of stock is meaningless. Although The Jazzy Jeweller sells for twice as much per share, its profits may also be twice as much per share — in which case The Jazzy Jeweller stock price may not be out of line given its profitability.

The level of a company's stock price relative to its earnings or profits per share helps you calibrate how expensively, cheaply, or fairly a stock price is valued. The formula is this:

Stock price per share ÷ Annual earnings per share = Price-to-earnings ratio

Over the long term, stock prices and corporate profits tend to move in sync, like good dance partners. The *price-to-earnings ratio*, or P/E ratio (say, "P E" — the slash isn't pronounced), compares the level of stock prices to the level of corporate profits, giving you a good sense of the stock's value. Over shorter periods of time, investors' emotions as well as fundamentals move stocks, but over longer terms, fundamentals have a far greater influence on stock prices.

P/E ratios can be calculated for individual stocks, as well as for entire stock indexes, portfolios, or funds.

Over the past 100-plus years, the P/E ratio of stocks has averaged around 15. During times of low inflation, the ratio tends to be higher — in the high teens to low 20s. The P/E ratio for U.S. stocks in 1999 got into the 30s, well above historic norms even for a period of low inflation. So, the down market that began in 2000 wasn't surprising, especially given the fall in corporate profits that put even more pressure on stock prices.

Just because stocks have historically averaged P/E ratios of about 15 doesn't mean that every individual stock will trade at such a P/E. Here's why: Suppose that you have a choice between investing in two companies, Superb Software and Tortoise Technologies. Say both companies' stocks sell at a P/E of 15. If Superb Software's business and profits grow 40 percent per year and Tortoise's business and profits remain flat, which would you buy?

Because both stocks trade at a P/E of 15, Superb Software appears to be the better buy. Even if Superb's stock continues to sell at 15 times its earnings, its stock price should increase 40 percent per year as its profits increase. Faster-growing companies usually command higher P/E ratios. Of course, this assumes that companies have earnings. It's much harder — and riskier — evaluating share prices where there are losses rather than earnings.

Just because a stock price or an entire country's stock market seems to be at a high price level doesn't necessarily mean that that particular stock or market is overpriced. Always compare the price of a stock to that company's profits per share or the overall market's price level to the overall corporate profits. The P/E ratio captures this comparison. Faster-growing and more-profitable companies generally sell for a premium — they have higher P/E ratios. Also note that future earnings, which are difficult to predict, influence stock prices more than current earnings, which are old news. Finally, keep in mind that a relatively low P/E ratio on a particular stock can be a possible warning sign of problems ahead.

How to Get Ready to Invest in Stocks

There's always a chorus of self-anointed gurus saying that you can make fat profits if you pick your own stocks. Unless you're extraordinarily lucky or unusually gifted at analyzing company and investor behaviour, you won't earn above-average returns if you select your own stocks.

Keep the amount that you dedicate to individual stock investments to a minimum — ideally, no more than 20 percent of your invested dollars. You should do such investing for the educational value and enjoyment that you derive from it, not because you smugly think you're as skilled as the best professional money managers.

Stock prices

Just about every major financial and news site on the Internet offers stock quotes for free as a lure to get you to visit the site.

To view a stock price quote online, all you need is the security's trading symbol (which you obtain by using the stock symbol lookup feature universally offered with online quote services). Some major newspapers and business papers print a listing of the prior day's stock prices, while some — notably the *Globe and Mail* — have one full page dedicated to this practice, despite how readily available the information is online. The *National Post* has a "Financial Post" section, which is worth its subscription value for that one page alone. This page of market data has streams of useful stock reports, including 52-week highs and lows as well as percent gainers and losers. Cable business channels, such as BNN, Bloomberg, and CNBC have stock quotes streaming across the bottom of the screen. You can stop by a local investment office and see the current stock quotes whizzing by on a long, narrow screen on a wall. Many investment firms also maintain publicly accessible terminals (that look a lot like personal computers) on which you can obtain current quotes.

The following table is a typical example of the kinds of information you can find in daily price quotes in papers and online; the quotes in this table are for the information technology giant International Business Machines (also known as Big Blue or IBM). The quote is from the New York Stock Exchange, so all the dollar figures are U.S. dollars. After the name of the company, you see the trading symbol, IBM, which is the code that you and brokers use to look up the price on computer-based quotation systems.

International Business Machines (IBM)	
52-wk range	172.19–211.98
Last trade	4:00 pm EST (196.47)
Change	+1.36 (+0.70%)
Day's range	194.35–196.86
Open	194.38
Volume	4,211,284
P/E ratio	13.4
Mkt cap	198.4B
Div/Shr	3.80
Yield	2.00%

Here's a breakdown of what the information in this table means:

- **52-wk range (52-week range):** These two numbers indicate the low ($172.19) and high ($211.98) trading prices for IBM during the past 52 weeks.

- **Last trade:** This line indicates the most recent price that the stock traded at (you can see that this IBM quote was from 4:00 p.m. Eastern Standard Time, which is when the New York Stock Exchange closes for the day).

- **Change:** This entry indicates how that price differs from the previous day's close. In this case, you can see that the stock was up $1.36 (0.70 percent) from the prior day's close.

- **Day's range:** These two numbers are the lowest and highest prices that the stock traded at during the day.

- **Open:** This line tells you the trade price closest to the market's open.

- **Volume:** This number indicates the number of shares that traded through this point in the trading day. (To conserve space, many newspapers indicate the volume in hundreds of shares — in other words, you must add two zeros to the end of the number to arrive at the actual number of shares.)

- **The P/E ratio:** As explained earlier in this chapter, the P/E ratio measures the price of IBM's stock relative to the company's earnings or profits.

- **Mkt cap (market capitalization):** This number tells you the current market value of all of IBM's stock, which in this case is $198.4 billion. You calculate this value by multiplying the current price per share by the total number of shares outstanding.

- **Div/Shr (dividends/share):** This number shows you the current dividend (in this case, $3.80 per share), which the company pays yearly to shareholders. Most companies actually pay out their annual dividends by distributing one-quarter of the total every three months.

- **Yield:** This number indicates the effective percentage yield that the stock's dividend produces. To calculate the effective yield, divide the dividend by the current stock price. In this example, IBM shareholders can expect to receive a dividend worth about 2 percent of the current stock price.

Stocks "direct" from companies

Numerous companies sell their stock directly to the public. Proponents of these direct stock purchase plans say that you can invest in stocks without paying any commissions. Well, the commission-free spiel isn't quite true, and investing in such plans poses other challenges.

If you want to purchase directly from Home Depot, for example, you need a minimum initial investment of $500. Buying stock "direct" isn't free; in the case of Home Depot, for example, you have to pay a $5 enrollment fee. Although that may not sound like much on a $500 investment, $5 represents 1 percent of your investment. For subsequent purchases, you pay 5 percent up to a maximum of $2.50 per purchase plus $0.05 per share.

If you want to sell your shares, you have to pay a fee to do that, too — $25 plus $0.15 per share. Overall, these fees compare to what you would pay to buy stock through a discount broker. In some cases, these fees are actually higher. For example, you can reinvest dividends at no cost through many discount brokers.

Some direct stock purchase plans entail even more hassle and cost than the type we just discussed. With other plans, you must buy your initial shares through a broker and then transfer your shares to the issuing company in order to buy more. Also, you can't pursue most direct stock purchase plans within retirement plans.

Every time you want to set up a stock purchase plan with a company, you must request and complete the company's application forms. If you go through the hassle of doing so, say, a dozen times, you're rewarded with a dozen statements on a regular basis from each individual company (and, perhaps, a matching set of 12 headaches). Frankly, because of this drawback alone, consider buying stock through a discount brokerage account that allows centralized purchasing and holding of various stocks as well as consolidated tax-reporting statements.

Trades through a broker

Unless you decide to buy stock directly, you generally need a broker. Discount brokers are the best way to go — they take your orders and charge far less than conventional brokerage firms, which generally pay their brokers on commission.

After you decide which discount broker you want to use, request (by phone or via the Internet) an account application package for the type of account that you desire (non-retirement, Registered Retirement Savings Plan [RRSP], Tax-Free Savings Account [TFSA], Registered Education Savings Plan [RESP], and so on). Complete the forms (call the firm's toll-free number or visit a branch office if you get stuck), and mail or take them back to the discounter. Many discount brokers, of course, now allow you to sign up online.

When you're ready to place an actual order to buy stock, you simply log in to your account or call the discount broker and explain what you want to do. You have two options:

- **Market order:** A *market order* instructs your broker to buy the amount of stock that you want (100 shares, for example) at the current and best (lowest) price available. With securities in which there's little trading or generally volatile price movements, market orders are a bit riskier. As a result, you may want to instead consider a limit order.

- **Limit order:** Alternatively, you can try to buy a desired stock at a specific price. For example, you can place a purchase order at $32.50 per share when the stock's last trade was $33 per share. This type of order is known as a *limit order* and is good until you cancel it. Don't try this tactic, because it requires you to hope and gamble that the stock drops a little before it rises. If the stock simply rises from its current price of $33 per share or drops to $32.55 before it makes a big move higher, you may kick yourself. If you think that the stock is a good buy for the long haul, go buy it with a market order. If you don't think it's a good buy, don't buy it.

One final word of advice: Try to buy stock in good-sized chunks, such as 100 shares. Otherwise, commissions gobble a large percentage of the small dollar amount that you invest. If you don't have enough money to build a diversified portfolio all at once, don't sweat it. Diversify over time. Purchase a chunk of one stock after you have enough money accumulated and then wait to buy the next stock until you've saved another chunk to invest.

4

Exploring Bonds

Lending investments are those in which you lend your money to an organization, such as a bank, company, or government, which typically pays you a set or fixed rate of interest. *Ownership investments,* by contrast, provide partial ownership of a company or some other asset, such as real estate, that has the ability to generate revenue and potential profits.

Investing in bonds, which are a type of lending investment, is a time-honoured way to earn a better rate of return on money that you don't plan to use within the next couple of years or more. This chapter notes when it makes sense to buy bonds, describes different types, and explains how to buy them.

Suitable Uses for Bonds

As with stocks, bonds can generally be sold any day that the financial markets are open. Because their values fluctuate, though, you're more likely to lose money if you're forced to sell your bonds sooner rather than later. In the short term, if the bond market happens to fall and you need to sell, you could lose money. In the longer term, as is the case with stocks, you're far less likely to lose money. You can also make profits by selling bonds at a higher price than you paid.

Don't put your emergency cash reserve into bonds — that's what a high-interest savings account, money market fund, or bank savings account is for. And don't put too much of your longer-term investment money into bonds, either. As explained in Chapter 1, bonds are generally inferior investments for making your money grow. Growth-oriented investments, such as stocks, real estate, and your own business, hold the greatest potential to build wealth.

Here are some common situations in which investing in bonds can make sense:

- **You're looking to make a major purchase.** This purchase should be one that won't happen for at least two years, such as buying a home or some other major expenditure. Shorter-term bonds may work for you as a higher-yielding and slightly riskier alternative to money market funds.

- **You want to diversify your portfolio.** Bonds don't move in tandem with the performance of other types of investments, such as stocks. In fact, in a terrible economic environment (such as during the Great Depression in the early 1930s or the financial crisis of 2008), bonds may appreciate in value while riskier investments, such as stocks, plunge.

- **You're interested in long-term investments.** You may invest some of your money in bonds as part of a longer-term investment strategy, such as for retirement. You should have an overall plan for how you want to invest your money, sometimes referred to as an *asset allocation strategy*. Aggressive, younger investors should keep less of their retirement money in bonds than older folks who are nearing retirement.

- **You need income-producing investments.** If you're retired or not working much, bonds can be useful because they're better at producing current income than many other investments.

Different Types of Bonds

Bonds differ from one another according to a number of factors — length (number of years) to maturity, credit quality, and the entities that issue the bonds. After you have a handle on these issues, you're ready to consider investing in individual bonds and bond mutual funds and exchange-traded funds (ETFs).

Unfortunately, due to shady marketing practices by some investing companies and salespeople who sell bonds, you can have your work cut out for you while trying to get a handle on what many bonds really are and how they differ from their peers. But don't worry. The following sections help you wade through the muddy waters.

Maturity matters

Maturity simply means the time at which the bond promises to pay back your principal — next year, in 7 years, in 15 years, and so on. A bond's maturity gives you a good (although far-from-perfect) sense of how volatile a bond may be if interest rates change. If interest rates fall, bond prices rise; if interest rates rise, bond prices fall. Longer-term bonds drop more in price when the overall level of interest rates rises.

Suppose you're considering investing in two bonds that the same organization issues, and both yield 7 percent. The bonds differ from one another only in when they'll mature: One is a two-year bond; the other is a 20-year bond. If interest rates were to rise just 1 percent (from 7 percent to 8 percent), the two-year bond may decline about 2 percent in value, whereas the 20-year bond could fall approximately five times as much — 10 percent.

If you hold a bond until it matures, you get your principal back, unless the issuer defaults. In the meantime, however, if interest rates rise, bond prices fall. The reason is simple: If the bond that you hold is issued at, say, 7 percent, and interest rates on similar bonds rise to 8 percent, no one (unless they don't know any better) wants to purchase your 7 percent bond. The value of your bond has to decrease enough so it effectively yields 8 percent.

Bonds are generally classified by the length of time until maturity:

- Short-term bonds mature in the next few years.
- Intermediate-term bonds come due within three to ten years.
- Long-term bonds mature in more than ten years, generally up to 30 years.

Although rare, a number of companies issue 100-year bonds! A number of railroads did, as did Coca-Cola, Disney,

IBM, the New York Port Authority, and the Government of China. And the Government of Canada has issued 50-year bonds. Such bonds are quite dangerous to purchase, especially if they're issued during a period of relatively low interest rates.

Most of the time, longer-term bonds pay higher yields than short-term bonds. You can look at a chart of the current yield of similar bonds plotted against when they mature — such a chart is known as a *yield curve*. Most of the time, this curve slopes upward. Investors generally demand a higher rate of interest for taking the risk of holding longer-term bonds.

The likelihood of default

In addition to being issued for various lengths of time, bonds differ from one another in the creditworthiness of the issuer. To minimize investing in bonds that default, purchase highly rated bonds. Credit-rating agencies such as Moody's, DBRS (originally Dominion Bond Rating Service), Standard & Poor's, and Fitch rate the credit quality and likelihood of default of bonds.

The *credit rating* of a bond depends on the issuer's ability to pay back its debt. Bond credit ratings are usually done on some sort of a letter-grade scale where, for example, AAA is the highest rating and ratings descend through AA and A, followed by BBB, BB, B, CCC, CC, C, and so on. Here's the lowdown on the ratings:

- **AAA- and AA-rated bonds** are considered *high-grade* or *high-credit-quality bonds.* Such bonds have little chance — a fraction of 1 percent — of default.

- **A- and BBB-rated bonds** are considered *investment-grade* or *general-quality bonds.*

- **BB- or lower-rated bonds** are known as *junk bonds* (or by their marketed name, *high-yield bonds*). Junk bonds, also known as *non-investment-grade bonds,* are more likely to default — perhaps as many as a couple of percent per year actually default.

Why would any sane investor buy a bond with a low credit rating? He or she may purchase one of these bonds because issuers pay a higher interest rate on lower-quality bonds to attract investors. The lower a bond's credit rating and quality, the higher the yield you can and should expect from such a bond. Poorer-quality bonds, though, aren't for the faint of heart because they're generally more volatile in value.

 Avoid buying individual junk bonds — consider investing in these bonds only through a well-run junk-bond fund.

Issuers (and tax implications)

In addition to varying in credit ratings and maturity, bonds differ from one another according to the type of organization that issues them — in other words, what kind of organization you lend your money to. The following sections go over the major options and tell you when each option may make sense for you.

Treasury bills

Treasury bills, or T-bills, are short-term government bonds available for terms of 3, 6, and 12 months. The federal government, as well as some provinces, issue T-bills in large denominations, but many financial institutions repackage them and make them available to the public in amounts as small as $1,000. You don't receive any interest when you own a T-bill. Instead, you purchase them at a discount to their face value. Your return — in effect, the interest you make — is the difference between your purchase price and the face value, which you receive at maturity. You'll see this return displayed as an interest rate by most financial institutions; they do this simply to help you assess the return you'll make.

Government of Canada bonds

Canada's biggest debtor of them all issues marketable bonds. These can be bought in denominations as low as $1,000. Government of Canada marketable bonds — like most bonds — are usually quoted as a price per $100 of the value at maturity of the bond. Interest on Government of Canada bonds is paid twice a year.

The best use of T-bills and Government of Canada bonds is in place of bank Guaranteed Investment Certificates (GICs). If you feel secure with the federal government insurance (which is limited to $100,000) that a bank GIC provides, check out a T-bill (which has the unlimited backing of the Canadian government) or federal marketable bond. Government of Canada bonds that mature in the same length of time as a GIC may pay the same interest rate, or better.

Canada Savings Bonds

The annual ad campaign for Canada Savings Bonds (CSBs) — usually with some colourful maple leaves getting a star turn — had almost become as expected as the turning of the leaves themselves as a signal that fall had arrived. CSBs were touted as the patriotic way to lend your money to the federal government. But even if you wanted to, you can't anymore.

In its March 2017 budget, the Government of Canada announced it would no longer be selling CSBs or Canada Premium Bonds (CPBs) as of November 2017. The reasons, the government said at the time, were the declining sales, the alternatives available to consumers, and the cost of administering and managing the program.

Any CSBs or CPBs not matured yet are still guaranteed by the government and will continue to earn interest until you redeem them or they mature, whichever comes first, and be repriced. Depending on the maturity date of the bond series, outstanding CSBs will cease paying interest no later than November 1 or December 1, 2021.

If you have funds in a Retirement Savings Plan (RSP), you can transfer them to another registered plan anytime you want. To make a transfer, you need to submit the proper form — the Canada Revenue Agency (CRA) Record of Direct Transfer Form T2033 or equivalent — completed by the financial institution where you want your money to go, or your RSP administrator. You can also withdraw money from your RSP, but you'll generally be hit by withholding taxes.

Municipal bonds

Municipal bonds are city and regional government bonds that pay interest. The rate is typically better than what you'd receive from other bonds with a similar maturity. They also usually offer a better rate than that paid by GICs with a comparable term. Unlike a GIC, though, you're not locked in, and you can sell them when you want.

Corporate bonds

Companies such as Bell, Domtar, and Sun Life issue corporate bonds. The later section "Bond prices" shows you how to read price listings for such bonds. If you buy corporate bonds through a mutual fund or an ETF, you don't need to price such bonds.

Mortgage bonds

Remember that mortgage you took out when you purchased your home? Well, you can actually purchase a bond, naturally called a *mortgage bond,* to invest in a portfolio of mortgages just like yours. Many banks actually sell their mortgages as bonds in the financial markets, which allows other investors to invest in them. The mortgages are bundled together and sold as mortgage-backed securities (MBSs). The Canada Mortgage and Housing Corporation, a government agency, usually guarantees repayment of principal on MBSs at the bond's maturity. MBSs are sometimes referred to as Cannie Maes, a play on Ginnie Maes, the nickname for the U.S. mortgage-backed securities called Government National Mortgage Association certificates.

 The vast majority of mortgage bonds are quite safe to invest in. The risky ones that were in the news in the late 2000s for defaulting were so-called subprime mortgages, which lacked government agency backing.

Convertible bonds

Convertible bonds are hybrid securities — they're bonds you can convert under a specified circumstance into a preset number of shares of stock in the company that issued the bond. Although these bonds do pay taxable interest, their yield is lower than nonconvertible bonds because convertibles offer you the potential to make more money if the underlying stock rises. Convertibles are listed on the stock exchange so you can buy or sell them with full transparency.

Inflation-protected Treasury bonds

The Canadian government offers bonds called *Government of Canada Real Return Bonds.* Compared with traditional Government of Canada bonds (which are discussed earlier in this chapter), the inflation-indexed bonds carry a lower interest rate.

The reason for this lower rate is that the other portion of your return with these inflation-indexed bonds comes from the inflation adjustment to the principal you invest. The inflation portion of the return gets added back into principal. For example, if you invest $10,000 in an inflation-indexed bond and inflation increases 3 percent the first year you hold the bond, your principal would increase to $10,300 at the end of the first year.

What's appealing about these bonds is that no matter what happens with the rate of inflation, investors who buy inflation-indexed bonds always earn some return (the yield or interest rate paid) above and beyond the rate of inflation. Thus, holders of inflation-indexed Treasury bonds can't have the purchasing power of their principal or interest eroded by high inflation.

Because inflation-indexed Treasury bonds protect the investor from the ravages of inflation, they represent a less risky security. However, consider this little-known fact: If the economy experiences *deflation* (falling prices), your principal isn't adjusted down, so these bonds offer deflation protection as well. As discussed in Chapter 1, lower risk usually translates into lower returns.

How to Buy Bonds

You can invest in bonds in one of two major ways: You can purchase individual bonds, or you can invest in a professionally selected and managed portfolio of bonds via a bond mutual fund or an ETF (see Chapter 5).

This section helps you decide how to invest in bonds. If you want to take the individual bond route, that path is covered here, and you find out how to decipher bond listings in financial newspapers or online. You can also learn about the purchasing process for T-bills (a different animal in that you can buy them directly from the government) and all other bonds. If you fall on the side of funds, head to Chapter 5 for more information.

Individual bonds versus bond funds

Unless the bonds you're considering purchasing are easy to analyze and homogeneous (such as Treasury bonds), you're generally better off investing in bonds through a mutual fund or an ETF. Here's why:

- **Diversification is more difficult with individual bonds.** You shouldn't put your money into a small number of bonds of companies in the same industry or that mature at the same time. It's difficult to cost-effectively build a diversified bond portfolio with individual issues, unless you have a substantial amount of money ($1 million) that you want to invest in bonds.

- **Individual bonds cost you more money.** If you purchase individual bonds through an investment advisor, you're going to pay a commission. In most cases, the commission cost is hidden — the broker quotes you a price for the bond that includes the commission. Even if you use a discount broker, these fees take a healthy bite out of your investment. The smaller the amount that you invest, the bigger the bite — on a $1,000 bond, the commission fee can equal several percent. Commissions take a smaller bite out of larger bonds — perhaps less than 0.5 percent if you use discount brokers.

  On the other hand, investing in bonds through a fund is cost-effective. Great actively managed bond funds are yours for less than 1 percent per year in operating expenses. And good bond index funds can be had for half that cost, or cheaper, if you choose a bond index fund. Selecting good bond funds isn't hard, as explained in Chapter 5.

- **You've got better things to do with your time.** Do you really want to research bonds and go bond shopping? Bonds are boring to most people. And bonds and the companies that stand behind them aren't that simple to understand. For example, did you know that some bonds can be called before their maturity dates? Companies often *call* bonds (which means they repay the principal and all accrued interest before maturity) to save money if interest rates drop significantly. After you purchase a bond, you need to do the same things that a good bond mutual fund portfolio manager needs to do, such as track the issuer's creditworthiness and monitor other important financial developments.

Bond prices

Business-focused publications and websites provide daily bond pricing. You may also call an investment dealer or browse websites to obtain bond prices. Table 4-1 illustrates a sample online bond listing from August 2018 for Bell Canada.

Issuer	Bond Type	Coupon Rate	Coupon Frequency	Maturity	Price	Yield	Yield Type	Duration	Sector Code
BELL CANADA	CORP	8.88	S	2026/04/17	136.97	4.25	M	7.05	CDNCORP

Table 4-1: *Sample Online Bond Listing*

Here's what each column means:

- **Issuer:** This column tells you who issued the bond. In this case, the issuer is a large telecommunications company, Bell Canada.

- **Bond Type:** Bell Canada's bond is, rightfully so, listed as a corporate bond. The other possible types include municipal, provincial, and federal government.

- **Coupon Rate:** This is the amount of interest paid per year expressed as a percentage value of the face value of the bond.

- **Coupon Frequency:** This refers to how often interest is paid out annually. The *S* in Table 4-1 stands for *semiannually.*

- **Maturity:** This states when the bondholder will have his or her principal paid back (year/month/day).

- **Price:** This shows the last price at which the bond traded.

- **Yield:** This tells you what the bond is currently yielding. It's calculated by dividing the original interest rate (the coupon rate) — 8.88 percent, in this example — by the current price per bond ($136.97). In addition, the yield also factors in the amortization of the difference between the bond's current price and its par value over the life of the bond. In this case, the yield equals 4.25 percent.

- **Yield Type:** The *M* in this column tells you the yield being calculated is the yield to *maturity.* (A *C* would indicate the yield is being calculated up to the date on which the bond can be bought back by the issuer, or *called.*)

  - **Duration:** This measures a bond's interest rate risk, using the bond's maturity, yield, coupon, and call features. It shows how long it will take for the price of a bond to be paid back with its internal cash flows. The result — a single number — is a measurement of how sensitive the bond's price is to interest rate changes. It's an important measurement, because bonds with higher durations carry more risk and have higher price volatility than bonds with lower durations.

- **Sector Code:** This tells you which type of issuer the bond comes from, such as a Canadian corporation or the Canadian government.

In addition to the direction of overall interest rates, changes in the financial health of the issuing entity that stands behind the bond strongly affect the price of an individual bond.

Guidelines for buying individual bonds

Purchasing different types of individual bonds (except for Government of Canada bonds), such as corporate and mortgage bonds, is a treacherous and time-consuming undertaking. Here's some advice for doing it right and minimizing the chance of mistakes:

- **Don't buy through salespeople.** Investment firms that employ representatives on commission are in the sales business. Many of the worst bond-investing disasters have befallen customers of such investment firms. Your best bet is to purchase individual bonds through discount brokers.

- **Don't be suckered into high yields — buy quality.** Yes, junk bonds pay higher yields, but they also have a much higher chance of default. Nothing personal, but you're not going to do as good a job as a professional money manager at spotting problems and red flags. Stick with highly rated bonds so you don't have to worry about and suffer through these consequences.

- **Understand that bonds may be called early.** Many bonds, especially corporate bonds, can legally be called before maturity. In this case, the bond issuer pays you back early because it doesn't need to borrow as much money or because interest rates have fallen and the borrower wants to reissue new bonds at a lower interest rate. Be especially careful about purchasing bonds that were issued at higher interest rates than those that currently prevail. Borrowers pay off such bonds first.

- **Diversify.** To buffer changes in the economy that adversely affect one industry or a few industries more than others, invest in and hold bonds from a variety of companies in different industries.

Of the money that you want to invest in bonds, don't put more than 5 percent into any one bond. That means you need to hold at least 20 bonds. Diversification requires a good amount to invest, given the size of most bonds and because trading fees erode your investment balance if you invest too little. If you can't achieve this level of diversification, use a bond mutual fund or an ETF (see Chapter 5).

- **Shop around.** Just as when you buy a car, shop around for good prices on the bonds that you have in mind. The hard part is doing an apples-to-apples comparison because different investment dealers may not offer the same exact bonds. Keep in mind that the two biggest determinants of what a bond should yield are its maturity date and its credit rating, both of which are discussed earlier in this chapter.

Unless you invest in boring, simple-to-understand bonds such as Government of Canada bonds, you're better off investing in bonds via the best bond mutual funds. One exception is if you absolutely, positively must receive your principal back on a certain date. Because bond funds don't mature, individual bonds with the correct maturity for you may best suit your needs. Consider Government of Canada bonds because they carry such a low default risk. Otherwise, you need a lot of time, money, and patience to invest well in individual bonds.

5

Mastering Mutual Funds and Exchange-Traded Funds

Different types of mutual funds and exchange-traded funds (ETFs) can help you meet various financial goals, which is why investors have more than $1.6 trillion invested in these funds. You can use money market funds for something most everybody needs: an emergency savings stash of three to six months' living expenses (although given the low interest rates over the last few years, in most cases you'll do better with a high-interest savings account). Or perhaps you're thinking about saving for a home purchase, retirement, or future educational costs. If so, you can consider some stock and bond funds. Because efficient funds take most of the hassle and cost out of deciding which companies to invest in, they're among the finest investment vehicles available today.

If you haven't taken a comprehensive look at your personal finances, read Chapter 2 to begin this important process. Too many people plunge into funds without looking at their overall financial situation and, in their haste, often end up paying more taxes and overlooking other valuable financial strategies.

Mutual Funds versus Exchange-Traded Funds

Mutual funds are big pools of money from investors that a fund manager uses to buy a bunch of stocks, bonds, and other assets that meet the fund's investment criteria.

ETFs are relatively new. The first one was created in 1993. They've gained more traction in recent years and now hold almost 10 percent of the total assets of the Canadian fund industry. ETFs are similar to mutual funds in that they also invest a pot of investors' money into stocks, bonds, and so on. The most significant difference is that in order to invest in an ETF, you must buy it through a stock exchange where ETFs trade, just as individual stocks trade. Thus, you need an investment account to invest in ETFs.

Most ETFs are also like index mutual funds (mentioned later in this chapter) in that each ETF generally tracks a major market index. (Beware that more and more companies are issuing ETFs that are actively traded or that track narrowly focused indexes such as an industry group or small country.) The best ETFs may also have slightly lower operating expenses than the lowest-cost index mutual funds. However, you must pay a commission to buy and sell an ETF, and the current market price of the ETF may deviate slightly from the underlying market value of the securities in its portfolio.

Regardless of whether you choose to invest in a mutual fund or an ETF, good funds enable you to have some of the best money managers in the country direct the investment of your money.

The Benefits of the Best Funds

The best funds are superior investment vehicles for people of all economic means, and they can help you accomplish many financial objectives. The following sections go over the main reasons for investing in funds rather than individual securities. (If you want to invest in individual stocks, Chapter 3 provides information on how best to do so.)

Professional management

The fund investment company hires a portfolio manager and researchers whose full-time jobs are to analyze and purchase suitable investments for the fund. These people screen the universe of investments for those that meet the fund's stated objectives.

Typically, fund managers are graduates of the top business and finance schools, where they learned portfolio management and securities valuation and selection. Many have additional investing credentials, such as being a Chartered Financial Analyst (CFA). In addition to their educational training, the best fund managers typically have ten or more years of experience in analyzing and selecting investments.

For most fund managers and researchers, finding the best investments is more than a full-time job. Fund managers do tons of analysis that you probably lack the time or expertise to perform. For example, fund managers assess company financial statements; interview a company's managers to get a sense of the company's business strategies and vision; examine competitor strategies; speak with company customers, suppliers, and industry consultants; attend trade shows; and read industry periodicals.

 In short, a fund management team does more research, number crunching, and due diligence than most people could ever have the energy or expertise to do in what little free time they have. Investing in funds frees up time for friendships, family relationships, hobbies, and more — don't miss the terrific time-saving benefits of fund investing.

Cost efficiency

Mutual funds and ETFs offer a cheaper, more communal way of getting your investment work done. When you invest your money in an efficiently managed fund, it likely costs you less than trading individual securities on your own. Fund managers can buy and sell securities for a fraction of the cost you pay and often for free.

Funds also spread the cost of research over thousands of investors. The most efficiently managed funds cost less than 1.5 percent per year in fees. (Bonds and money market funds cost much less — in the neighbourhood of 1 percent per year or less.) Some of the larger and more established funds can charge annual fees of less than 0.75 percent per year — that's less than a $7.50 annual charge per $1,000 you invest.

Diversification

Diversification is a big attraction for many investors who choose funds. Most funds own stocks or bonds from dozens of companies, thus diversifying against the risk of bad news from any single company or sector. Achieving such diversification on your own is difficult and expensive unless you have a few hundred thousand dollars and a great deal of time to invest.

Funds typically invest in 25 to 100 securities or more. Proper diversification increases the fund's chances of earning higher returns with less risk.

Although most funds are diversified, some aren't. For example, some stock funds invest exclusively in stocks of a single industry (for example, retailers) or a developing country (such as Mexico). Consider avoiding these funds because of the narrowness of their investments and their typically higher operating fees.

Reasonable investment minimums

Most funds have low minimum investment requirements. Many funds have minimums of $500 or less. Retirement plan investors can often invest with even less. Some funds even offer monthly investment plans so you can start with as little as $50 per month.

Even if you have lots of money to invest, you should consider funds. Increasing numbers of fund companies offer their higher-balance customers special funds with lower annual operating expenses and, thus, even better returns.

Different funds for different folks

Some people think that funds = stock market investing = risky. This line of thinking is wrong. The majority of money in funds isn't in the stock market. You can select the funds that take on the kinds of risks that you're comfortable with and that meet your financial goals. Here are the three major types of funds:

- **Stock funds:** If you want your money to grow over a long period of time (and you can handle down as well as up years), choose funds that invest more heavily in stocks.

- **Bond funds:** If you need current income and don't want investments that fluctuate as widely in value as stocks do, consider bond funds.

- **Money market funds:** If you want to be sure that your invested principal doesn't decline in value because you may need to use your money in the short term, select a money market fund.

Most investors choose a combination of these three types of funds to diversify and help accomplish different financial goals.

High financial safety

Thousands of banks and insurance companies — the vast majority in the United States — have failed in recent decades.

Banks and insurers can fail when their *liabilities* (the money that customers gave them to invest, which may need to be returned on short notice) can exceed their *assets* (the money that they've invested or lent).

For example, when big chunks of a bank's loans go sour at the same time that its depositors want their money, the bank fails; banks typically have less than $0.15 on deposit for every dollar that their customers place with them. Likewise, if an insurance company makes several poor investments or under-estimates the number of insurance policyholder claims, it, too, can fail.

Such failures can't happen with a mutual fund or ETF because the value of the fund's shares fluctuates as the securities in the fund rise and fall in value. For every dollar of securities they hold for their customers, funds have a dollar's worth of securities. The worst that can happen with a fund is that if you want your money, you may get less money than you originally put into the fund due to a market value decline of the fund's holdings — but you won't lose all your original investment.

For added security, the specific stocks, bonds, and other securities that a fund buys are held at a *custodian,* a separate organization independent of the fund company. A custodian ensures that the fund management company can't embezzle your funds or use assets from a better-performing fund to subsidize a poor performer.

Accessibility

What's really terrific about dealing with funds is that they're set up for people who value their time and don't like going to a local branch office and standing in long lines. With fund investing, you can fill out a simple form (often online) and write a cheque in the comfort of your home (or authorize electronic transfers from your bank or other accounts) to make your initial investment. You can then typically make subsequent investments by mailing in a cheque or zapping in money electronically.

Many fund companies also allow you to electronically transfer money back and forth from your local bank or credit union account; you can access your money almost as quickly through a money market fund as you can through your local bank.

Selling shares of your funds is usually simple. Generally, all you need to do is call the fund company's toll-free number or visit its website. Some companies have representatives available around the clock, year-round. Most fund companies also offer online account access and trading capabilities as well (although some people are prone to overtrading online, so beware).

The Keys to Successful Fund Investing

This chapter helps explain why mutual funds and ETFs are good investment vehicles to use. However, keep in mind that not all funds are worthy of your investment dollars. Would you, for example, invest in a fund run by an inexperienced and unproven 18-year-old? How about a fund that charges high fees and produces inferior returns in comparison to similar funds? You don't have to be an investing wizard to know the correct answers to these questions.

When you select a fund, you can use a number of simple, common-sense criteria to greatly increase your chances of investment success. The criteria presented in the following sections have been proven to dramatically increase your fund investing returns.

Minimize costs

The charges that you pay to buy or sell a fund, as well as the ongoing fund operating expenses, can have a big impact on the rate of return that you earn on your investments. Because hundreds of choices are available for a particular type of fund (larger-company Canadian stock funds, for example), you have no reason to put up with inflated costs.

Fund costs are an important factor in the return that you earn from a fund because fees are deducted from your investment returns and can attack a fund from many angles. All other things being equal, high fees and other charges depress your returns.

Stick with funds that maintain low total operating expenses and that don't charge *sales loads* (commissions). Both types of fees come out of your pocket and reduce your rate of return. Plenty of excellent funds are available with reasonable management expense fees (less than 2 percent for stock funds; less than 1 percent for bond funds).

Understand different fees

Mutual funds are a business. And like most businesses, they like to make a profit. Here's how they do it and how you pay for it.

Every mutual fund charges all investors in the fund a fee for the services of the manager. This is called the *management fee.* The management fee is calculated as a percentage of the total dollar value of the assets in the fund. This fee also includes money that is paid out each year to the advisor, dealer, or brokerage that sold you the fund. This fee is called a *trailing commission* or *trailer.* Charging you a trailing commission is usually defended as being a justifiable payment to the advisor for the services and advice they supposedly offer you on an ongoing basis. But the reality is that often once you buy a fund, you receive little — if any — true service for this fee, a fee many funds make mandatory. The reality is that the function of trailing commissions is to "encourage" you to keep your money invested in that particular fund and not move it to another fund.

In addition to the management fee, fund companies also pass along their operating costs, including but not limited to day-to-day operating expenses (which includes record keeping, fund valuation costs, and audit and legal fees), as well as the costs of sending out prospectuses and annual reports. Finally, they tack on taxes.

Added together, these three different fees — the management fee, the operating costs, and taxes — are known as the management expenses. However, you'll typically only hear reference to the *management expense ratio* (MER). The reason is that, similar to the basic management fee, the amount of the management expenses charged by a fund are a percentage of the total value of the fund's assets.

MERs are tremendously important to you as an investor. The higher they are, the less your investment earns you. By way of illustration, a 2 percent MER may sound quite reasonable, if not a downright bargain. But the money is paid out of the profits the fund earns in the year. So, if a fund made a gross return of 8 percent on its investments over the year, and charged a 2 percent MER, you would only earn 6 percent. Put another way, the mutual fund company is pocketing a full 25 percent of the fund's gains.

Contrast that with a fund with a low MER of just 0.5 percent, such as an index fund or ETF, that rang up the same gross return of 8 percent. Deducting its 0.5 percent MER, the low-cost fund would leave you with a return of 7.5 percent. At the risk of this becoming a math class, the lower MER fund, by giving you a return of 7.5 percent, compared to the high-cost fund's return of 6 percent, gives you an extra profit of 1.5 percent. In other words, the low-cost fund provides you with a 25 percent higher return than the high-cost fund.

Avoid load funds

You need to minimize the *sales load*, which is a commission paid to brokers and financial planners who work on commission and sell mutual funds. Commissions, or *loads*, generally range up to 6 percent of the amount that you invest. Sales loads are an additional and unnecessary cost that's deducted from your investment money. You can find plenty of outstanding *no-load* (commission-free) funds.

Advisors, being advisors, sing the praises of buying a load fund, warn against no-loads, and sometimes even try to obscure the load. For example, advisors may tell you that the commission doesn't cost you because the mutual fund company pays it. Keep in mind that the commission *always* comes out of your investment dollars, regardless of how cleverly some load funds and advisors disguise the commission.

Brokers and financial planners may also say that load funds perform better than no-load funds. One reason, they claim, is that load funds supposedly hire better fund managers. Absolutely no relationship exists between paying a sales charge to buy a fund and gaining access to better investment managers. The sales commission goes to the selling investment advisor, not to the fund managers. Objective studies demonstrate time and again that load funds not only don't outperform but, in fact, underperform no-loads. Common sense suggests why: When you factor in the higher commissions and the higher average ongoing operating expenses charged on load funds, you pay more to own a load fund, so your returns are less.

Another problem with commission-driven, load-fund sellers is the power of self-interest. This issue is rarely talked about, but it's even more important than the extra costs that you pay with load funds. When you buy a load fund through a salesperson, you miss out on the chance to get holistic advice on other personal finance strategies. For example, you may be better off paying down your debts or investing in something entirely different from a mutual fund. But salespeople almost never advise you to pay off your credit cards or your mortgage — or to invest through your company's retirement plan or in real estate — instead of buying an investment through them.

Some mutual fund companies try to play it both ways. They sell load funds (through brokers/advisors) as well as no-load funds (direct to investors). Be aware of this when a "financial advisor" says he can get you into funds from the leading companies because what he really may be telling you is that he's pitching load funds.

Unfortunately, some fund companies have crafty ways of hiding sales loads. Advisors and financial planners sell funds that they call no-loads, but these funds aren't no-loads.

With *back-end* or *deferred sales* load funds, the commission is hidden, thanks to the different classes of shares, known as A, B, C, and D classes. Salespeople tell you that as long as you stay in a fund for five to seven years, you need not pay the back-end sales charge that applies when you sell the investment. This claim may be true, but it's also true that these funds pay investment salespeople a hefty commission. (The Canadian Securities Administrators has proposed prohibiting such *deferred sales charges* [*DSCs*], but when — or even if — that will become official is as yet unknown.)

The salespeople can receive their commissions because the fund company charges you exorbitant continuing operating expenses (which are usually at least 1 percent more per year than the best funds). So, one way or another, they get their commissions from your investment dollars.

Beware of high operating expenses

In addition to loads, the other costs of owning funds are the ongoing *operating expenses.* All funds charge fees as long as you keep your money in the fund. The fees pay for the costs of running a fund, such as employees' salaries, marketing, toll-free phone lines, designing and distributing *prospectuses* (legal disclosure of the fund's operations and fees), and so on.

A fund's operating expenses are essentially invisible to you because they're deducted from the fund's share price. Companies charge operating expenses on a daily basis, so you don't need to worry about trying to get out of a fund at a particular time of the year before the company deducts these fees.

Although operating expenses are invisible to you, their impact on your returns is quite real. Studying the expenses of various money market funds and bond funds is critical; these funds buy securities that are so similar and so efficiently priced in the financial markets that most fund managers in a given type of money market or bond fund earn quite similar returns before expenses.

With stock funds, expenses may play less of an important role in your fund decision. However, don't forget that, over time, stocks have averaged returns of about 9 percent per year. So, if one stock fund charges 1 percent more in operating expenses than another and your expected long-term return is about 9 percent per year, you give up an extra 11 percent of your expected (pretax) annual returns (and an even greater portion of your after-tax returns).

All types of funds with higher operating expenses tend to produce lower rates of return on average. Conversely, funds with lower operating costs can more easily produce higher returns for you than a comparable type of fund with high costs. This effect makes sense because companies deduct operating expenses from the returns that your fund generates. Higher expenses mean a lower return to you.

Fund companies quote a fund's operating expenses as a percentage of your investment. The percentage represents an annual fee or charge. You can find this number in a fund's prospectus, in the fund expenses section, usually in a line that says something like "Total Fund Operating Expenses." You also can call the fund's toll-free number and ask a representative, or you can find the information at the fund company's website. Make sure that a fund doesn't appear to have low expenses simply because it's temporarily waiving them. (You can ask the fund representative or look at the fees in the fund's prospectus to find this information.)

Reflect on performance and risk

A fund's historical rate of return or performance is another important factor to weigh when you select a fund. However, keep in mind that, as all fund materials must tell you, past performance is no guarantee of future results. In fact, many former high-return funds achieved their results only by taking on high risk or simply by relying on short-term luck. Funds that assume higher risk should produce higher rates of return. But high-risk funds usually decline in price faster during major market declines. Thus, a good fund should consistently deliver a favourable rate of return given the level of risk that it takes.

A big mistake that many investors make when they choose a fund is overemphasizing the importance of past performance numbers. The shorter the time period you analyze, the greater the danger that you'll misuse high performance as an indicator for a good future fund.

Although past performance *can* be a good sign, high returns for a fund, relative to its peers, are largely possible only if a fund takes more risk (or if a fund manager's particular investment style happens to come into favour for a few years). The danger of taking more risk is that it doesn't always work the way you'd like. The odds are high that you won't be able to pick the next star before it vaults to prominence in the investing sky. You have a far greater chance of getting onboard when a recently high-performing fund is ready to plummet back to Earth.

One clever way fund managers make their funds look better is to compare them to funds that aren't really comparable. The most common ploy is for a manager to invest a fund in riskier types of securities and then compare its performance to funds that invest in less risky securities. Examine the types of securities that a fund invests in, and then make sure that the comparison funds or indexes invest in similar securities.

Also, firms will often merge funds, grafting a fund with poor performance onto one with strong returns. This essentially makes a badly managed fund disappear from the fund company's lineup . . . and from its marketing literature. Even if the managers did start — and sustain — a new, winning strategy, it would take a very, very long time for the fund's performance history to come out from under the shadow of a lousy three- or five-year track record.

What's more, a fund with dreadful returns brings down the overall return of investors who may hold that fund along with several others from the same company. Perhaps more important — from the fund company's perspective — a stinker fund sticks out, and makes it tougher to sell prospects on their purported investing know-how. This merge-and-disappear trick is often used on flavour-of-the-month funds that try to jump on an investment or theme that's making the headlines, such as cannabis stocks or cryptocurrencies. Often, by the time such funds are up and running, the air has come out of that particular bubble, and the future looks to only promise worse returns.

Stick with experience

A great deal of emphasis is placed on who manages a specific fund. Although the individual fund manager is important, a manager isn't an island unto himself. The resources and capabilities of the parent company are equally if not more important. Managers come and go, but fund companies usually don't.

Different companies maintain different capabilities and levels of expertise with different types of funds. Phillips, Hager & North (owned by the Royal Bank of Canada), for example, is terrific at money market, bond, and dividend stock funds, thanks in part to its low operating expenses. Fidelity and Templeton have significant experience with investing in international stocks.

A fund company gains more or less experience than others not only from the direct management of certain fund types but also through hiring out. For example, some fund families contract with private money management firms that possess significant experience. In other cases, private money management firms, such as Leith Wheeler Investment Counsel, Mawer Investment Management, and Steadyhand Investment Funds, offer mutual funds.

Consider index funds

Index funds are funds that are mostly managed by a computer. Unlike other funds, in which the portfolio manager and a team of analysts scour the market for the best securities, an index fund manager simply invests to match the makeup, and thus also the performance, of an index — a basket of stocks representing the performance of a stock market — such as the S&P/TSX Composite Index of the largest companies on the Toronto Stock Exchange. Most ETFs (see the earlier section "Mutual Funds versus Exchange-Traded Funds") are simply index funds that trade on a stock exchange.

Index funds deliver relatively good returns by keeping expenses low, staying invested, and not trying to jump around. Over ten years or more, index funds typically outperform about three-quarters of their peers. Most so-called actively managed funds can't overcome the handicap of high operating expenses that pull down their rates of return. Index funds can run with far lower operating expenses because significant ongoing research isn't needed to identify companies to invest in.

Many actively managed stock funds have management expense ratios (MERs) of 2 percent to 3 percent or higher. Index funds — and ETFs that track a corresponding stock market index — will typically have MERs of less than 1 percent. (See the earlier section "Understand different fees" for more on MERs.)

With actively managed stock funds, a fund manager can make costly mistakes, such as not being invested when the market goes up, being too aggressive when the market plummets, or just being in the wrong stocks. An actively managed fund can easily underperform the overall market index that it's competing against.

Don't try to pick *in advance* one of the few elite money managers who manage to beat the market averages by a few percentage points per year. Also, don't overestimate the pros' ability to consistently pick the right stocks. Index funds make sense for a portion of your investments, especially when you invest in bonds and larger, more conservative stocks, where beating the market is difficult for portfolio managers.

In addition to having lower operating expenses, which help boost your returns, index mutual funds and ETFs based upon an index are usually tax-friendlier when you invest outside retirement plans. Fund managers of actively managed portfolios, in their attempts to increase returns, buy and sell securities more frequently. However, this trading increases a fund's taxable capital gains distributions and reduces a fund's after-tax return.

Steer clear of leveraged and inverse exchange-traded funds

Since their introduction in 2006, leveraged and inverse ETFs have taken in tens of billions in assets. Here's the lowdown on these funds:

- **Leveraged ETFs:** These funds claim to magnify the move of a particular index, such as the Standard & Poor's (S&P) 500 stock index, by double or even triple in some cases. So, a double-leveraged S&P 500 ETF is supposed to increase by 2 percent for a 1 percent increase in the S&P 500 index.

- **Inverse ETFs:** These funds are supposed to move in the opposite direction of a given index. For example, an inverse S&P 500 ETF is supposed to increase by 1 percent for a 1 percent decrease in the S&P 500 index.

The steep 2008 decline in stock market indexes around the globe and the increasing volatility in that year created the perfect environment for leveraged and inverse ETFs. With these new vehicles, you could easily make money from major stock market indexes when they were falling. Or if you were convinced a particular index or industry group was about to zoom higher, you could buy a leveraged ETF that would magnify market moves by double or even triple.

Suppose back in early 2008, when the Dow Jones Industrial Average had declined about 10 percent from its then-recent peak above 14,000, you were starting to get nervous and wanted to protect your portfolio from a major market decline. You bought some of the ProShares UltraShort Dow 30 ETF (trading symbol DXD), which is an inverse ETF designed to move twice as much in the opposite direction of the Dow. If the Dow goes down, DXD goes up twice as much, and you make money.

Now consider what happened when you held on to the ETF through early 2010 — two years after you bought the fund in early 2008. Over this entire two-year period, the Dow was down about 20 percent. Your original thinking that the market was going to fall proved to be correct. If the ETF did what it was supposed to do and moved twice as much in the other direction, it should've increased 40 percent in value over this period, thus giving you a tidy return. But it didn't. It wasn't even close. The ETF actually plummeted nearly 50 percent in value over this two-year period.

Investigations of whether the leveraged (and inverse) ETFs actually deliver on their objectives show that they don't. In recent years, ETF issuers have come out with increasingly risky and costly ETFs. Leveraged and inverse ETFs are especially problematic in that regard. And the issuers of these leveraged and inverse ETFs got in trouble for their poor disclosure and misleading marketing. Buried in the fine print of the prospectuses of these ETFs, you usually see notes that these ETFs are designed to accomplish their stated objectives for only one trading day. As a result, they're really suitable only for day traders. Of course, few investors read (and understand) the dozens of pages of legal boilerplate in a prospectus.

Investment firms and industry regulators are taking notice of these problems. The Financial Industry Regulatory Authority (FINRA), the largest independent regulator for U.S. securities firms, issued a lengthy warning to financial advisors that "inverse and leveraged ETFs that are reset daily typically are unsuitable for retail investors who plan to hold them for longer than one trading session, particularly in volatile markets."

Retail investors pumped billions of dollars into leveraged and inverse ETFs without FINRA's clear explanation and disclosure. If they had, and if they had known how poorly these ETFs actually do over extended periods of time, they wouldn't have invested.

A number of investment firms have suspended trading in these ETFs. They're worried about their legal exposure, as well about what will happen if their customers invest in leveraged and inverse ETFs and get burned.

Leveraged and inverse ETFs aren't investments. They're gambling instruments for day traders. As an individual investor, if you happen to guess correctly before a short-term major market move, you may do well over a short period of time (longer than one day but no more than a few months). However, the odds are heavily stacked against you. You can reduce risk and hedge yourself through sensible diversification. If, for example, you don't want 80 percent of your portfolio exposed to stock market risk, invest a percentage you're comfortable with and don't waste your time and money with leveraged and inverse ETFs.

How to Create Your Fund Portfolio with Asset Allocation

Asset allocation simply means that you decide what percentage of your investments you place — or allocate — into bonds versus stocks and into U.S. and international stocks versus Canadian stocks. (Asset allocation can also include other assets, such as real estate and small business, which are discussed in Chapters 6 and 7.)

When you invest money for the longer term, such as for retirement, you can choose among the various types of funds that are discussed in this chapter. Most people get a big headache when they try to decide how to spread their money among the choices. This section helps you begin cutting through the clutter.

Allocate for the long term

Many working folks have time on their side, and they need to use that time to make their money grow. You may have two or more decades before you need to draw on some portion of your retirement account assets. If some of your investments drop a bit over a year or two — or even over five years — the value of your investments has plenty of time to recover before you spend the money in retirement.

Your current age and the number of years until you retire are the biggest factors in your allocation decision. The younger you are and the more years you have before retirement, the more comfortable you should be with volatile, growth-oriented investments, such as stock funds. (See Chapter 1 for the risks and historic returns of different investments.)

Table 5-1 lists guidelines for allocating fund money that you've earmarked for long-term purposes such as retirement. You don't need an MBA or PhD to decide your asset allocation — all you need to know is how old you are and the level of risk that you desire.

Your Investment Attitude	Bond Fund Allocation (%)	Stock Fund Allocation (%)
Play it safe	= Age	= 100 – Age
Middle of the road	= Age – 10	= 110 – Age
Aggressive	= Age – 20	= 120 – Age

Table 5-1: *Asset Allocation for the Long Haul*

What does it all mean, you ask? Consider this example: If you're a conservative sort who doesn't like a lot of risk, but you recognize the value of striving for some growth to make your money work harder, you're a middle-of-the-road type. Using Table 5-1, if you're 35 years old, you may consider putting 25 percent (35 − 10) into bond funds and 75 percent (110 − 35) into stock funds.

Now divvy up your stock investment money between Canadian and international funds. Here's what portion of your stock allocation you can consider investing in overseas stocks:

- 20 percent (for a play-it-safe attitude)
- 35 percent (for a middle-of-the-road attitude)
- 50 percent (for an aggressive attitude)

Using Table 5-1, if a 35-year-old, middle-of-the-road investor puts 75 percent in stocks, she can then invest about 35 percent of the stock fund investments (which works out to be around 25 percent of the total) in international stock funds. Here's what the 35-year-old, middle-of-the-road investor's portfolio asset allocation looks like:

Bonds	25%
Canadian stocks	50%
International stocks	25%

Diversify your stock fund investments

Suppose that your investment allocation decisions suggest that you invest 50 percent in Canadian stock funds. Which ones do you choose? Stock funds differ on a number of levels. You can choose from growth-oriented stocks and funds and those that focus on value stocks, as well as from funds that focus on small-, medium-, or large-company stocks. You also need to decide what portion you want to invest in index funds (which are discussed earlier in the section "Consider index funds") versus actively managed funds that try to beat the market.

 Generally, it's a good idea to diversify using different types of funds. You can diversify in one of two ways:

- **Purchase several individual funds, each of which focuses on a different style.** For example, you can invest in a large-company value stock fund and in a small-company growth fund. This approach is somewhat tedious. Granted, it does allow a fund manager to specialize and gain greater knowledge about a particular type of stock. But many of the best managers invest in more than one narrow range of security.

- **Invest in a handful of funds (five to ten), each of which covers several bases and that together cover them all.** Keep in mind that the investment delineations are somewhat arbitrary, and most funds focus on more than just one type of investment. For example, a fund may focus on small-company value stocks but may also invest in medium-company stocks. It may also invest in some that are more growth oriented.

Deciding how much you should use index versus actively managed funds is really a matter of personal taste. If you're satisfied knowing that you'll get the market rate of return and that you can't underperform the market (after accounting for your costs), index your entire portfolio. On the other hand, if you enjoy the challenge of trying to pick the better managers and want the potential to earn better than the market level of returns, don't use index funds at all. Investing in a happy medium of both is always a safe bet.

If you haven't experienced the sometimes-significant plummets in stock prices that occur, you may feel queasy the next time it happens and you've got a chunk of your nest egg in stocks. Be sure to read Chapters 1 and 3 to understand the risk in stocks and what you can and can't do to reduce the volatility of your stock holdings.

6

Investing in a Home

For most people, buying a home in which to live is their first, best, and only real estate investment. Homes may require a lot of financial feeding, but over the course of your life, owning a home (instead of renting) can make and save you money. Although the pile of mortgage debt seems daunting in the years just after your purchase, someday your home's *equity* (the market value of the home minus the outstanding mortgage debt) may be among your biggest assets.

 And, yes, real estate is still a good investment despite its declines in the late 2000s in some areas. Like stocks, real estate does well over the long term but doesn't go continuously higher. Smart investors take advantage of down periods; they consider these periods to be times to buy at lower prices just as they do when their favourite retailers are having a sale.

The Buying Decision

The decision of when — and if — to buy a home can be complex. Money matters, but so do personal and emotional issues. Buying a home is a big deal — you're settling down. Can you really see yourself coming home to this same place day after day, year after year? Of course, you can always move, but doing so, especially within just a few years of purchasing a home, can be costly and cumbersome, and now you've got a financial obligation to deal with.

The pros and cons of ownership

Some people — particularly enthusiastic salespeople in the real estate business — believe everybody should own a home. You may hear them say things like "Buy a home for the tax breaks" or "Renting is like throwing your money away."

As discussed later in this chapter, it's true that the profit you make when you sell the home in which you've been living — your *principal residence* — is tax-free. However, many

people end up living in their home for many, many years —
perhaps for the rest of their lives — while others use all the
profits from one home along with extra savings in order to
buy a larger property as their family grows. Tax-free profits are
great, but they often don't get redirected to your retirement or
other investment plan. Don't buy a home just because of the
tax break.

Also, renting isn't necessarily equal to "throwing your
money away." In fact, renting can have a number of benefits,
such as the following:

- **In some communities, with a given type of property,
  renting is less costly than buying.** Happy and successful renters include people who pay low rent, perhaps
  because they've made housing sacrifices. If you can
  sock away 10 percent or more of your earnings while
  renting, you're probably well on your way to accom-
  plishing your future financial goals.

- **You can save money and hopefully invest in other
  financial assets.** Stocks (see Chapter 3), bonds (see
  Chapter 4), and mutual funds and exchange-traded
  funds (see Chapter 5) are quite accessible and useful
  in retirement. Some long-term homeowners, by contrast, have a substantial portion of their wealth tied up
  in their homes. (Accessibility is a double-edged sword

because it may tempt you as a cash-rich renter to blow the money in the short term.)

- **Renting has potential emotional and psychological rewards.** The main reward is the not-so-inconsequential fact that you have more flexibility to pack up and move on. You may have a lease to fulfill, but you may be able to renegotiate it if you need to move on. As a home-owner, you have a major monthly payment to take care of. To some people, this responsibility feels like a financial ball and chain. After all, you have no guarantee that you can sell your home in a timely fashion or at the price you desire if you want to move.

Although renting has its benefits, renting has at least one big drawback: exposure to inflation. As the cost of living increases, your landlord can keep increasing your rent, even if you're protected by rent control. If you're a homeowner, however, the big monthly expense of the mortgage payment doesn't increase during the existing term of your mortgage, assuming that it's a fixed-rate mortgage. (Your property taxes, homeowner's insurance, and maintenance expenses are exposed to inflation, but these expenses are usually much smaller in comparison to your monthly mortgage payment or rent.)

Transaction costs

Financially speaking, you should wait to buy a home until you can see yourself staying put for a minimum of three years. Ideally, you should have a good shot of staying in the home for five or more years. Why? Buying and selling a home cost big bucks, and you generally need at least five years of low appreciation to recoup your transaction costs. Some of the expenses you face when buying and selling a home include the following:

- **Inspection fees:** You shouldn't buy a property without thoroughly checking it out, so you'll incur inspection expenses. Good inspectors can help you identify problems with the plumbing, heating, and electrical systems. They also check out the foundation, roof, and so on. They can even tell you whether termites are living in the house. Property inspections typically cost anywhere from a few hundred dollars up to $700 or more for larger homes.

- **Appraisal fee:** Your lender may require you to get your home appraised so that it can have an independent assessment of the home's value. An appraisal typically costs $300 to $600 or more.

- **Legal fees:** Although you can prepare an offer to purchase yourself and tend to the closing costs, using a lawyer to at least search the title is usually advisable.

A title search is carried out to determine that the vendor actually owns the home and has the right to sell it to you, and that the property doesn't have any claims against it. You can save some money by using a paralegal, but it's generally best to use a lawyer.

Despite a string of supposedly factual articles online and in newspapers, the majority of provinces do not require you to use a lawyer to complete the purchase. Using a lawyer, however, gives you valuable insurance. If the lawyer certifies that the seller has the right to sell you the property and that it doesn't have any claims against it — known as *free and marketable title* — and this later proves to be wrong, you can pursue a claim against the lawyer.

- **Title insurance:** When you buy a home, you and your lender need to protect yourselves against the chance — albeit small — that the property seller doesn't actually legally own the home you're buying. That's where title insurance comes in — it protects you financially from unscrupulous sellers. Title insurance costs vary by area, and can range from around $300 to $800 or more.

- **Moving costs:** You can transport all your furniture, clothing, and other personal belongings yourself, but your time is worth something, and your moving skills may be limited. Besides, do you want to end up in a hospital emergency room after being pinned at the bottom of a staircase by a runaway couch? Moving costs vary wildly, but you can count on spending hundreds to thousands of dollars. (You can get a ballpark idea of moving costs from a number of online calculators.)

- **Realtors' commissions:** A commission of 5 percent to 7 percent of the purchase price of most homes is paid to the real estate salespeople and the companies they work for. Higher-priced homes generally qualify for lower commission rates.

When buying a condo, you may also have to pay into a contingency reserve fund. (In some areas, including British Columbia, this is referred to as a *strata fund*.) This money is for covering repairs and upgrades that occur infrequently, such as upgrading elevators, repaving a road or parking lot, or replacing a roof. Sometimes condo owners are hit with a request for a large payment called a *special assessment*, which can range from a few thousand dollars to $80,000 or more. Many councils and boards charged with maintaining a healthy fund don't actually collect enough in monthly fees to cover these costs. Of course, when you're shopping for a condo, it's nice to see lower regular fees. But those fees may be attractive only because of poor forecasting or because the building is new and maintenance needs are low. When assessing a condo, ask for and go through the latest reserve fund report and plan from the condo corporation. Try to determine if the fund is sufficiently large enough to cover future needed repairs and replacements. If it doesn't appear to be, ask what the condo board's plans are for making up the shortfall.

Real estate advice on the web is some of the most error-prone and often simply wrong information in the personal finance world. The reason? Plain and simple, it's the big bucks involved. Consider that a 6 percent commission on a million-dollar property — far from uncommon in big cities — alone adds up to $60,000. You'll also find plenty of advice about the need to use lawyers — who regularly charge steep fees for what, in many cases, largely involves cutting and pasting and filling in standard forms using a computer programs, often done by clerical staff. Numerous articles explicitly state that a lawyer is required to buy a house, which as noted earlier, just is not the case in most provinces.

On top of all these transaction costs of buying and then selling a home, you'll also face maintenance expenses — for example, fixing leaky pipes and roofs as well as painting.

To cover all the transaction and maintenance costs of home ownership, the value of your home needs to appreciate about 15 percent over the years that you own it for you to be as well off financially as if you had continued renting. Fifteen percent! If you need or want to move elsewhere in a few years, counting on that kind of appreciation in those few years is risky. If you happen to buy just before a sharp rise in housing prices, you may get this much appreciation in a short time. But you can't count on this upswing — you're more likely to lose money on such a short-term deal.

Some people invest in real estate even when they don't expect to live in the home for long, and they may consider turning their home into a rental if they move within a few years. Doing so can work well financially in the long haul, but don't underestimate the responsibilities that come with rental property.

How Much Should You Spend?

Buying a home is a long-term financial commitment. You'll probably choose to repay the money you borrow to purchase your home (your *mortgage*) over 25 years. This is called the *amortization*. Your home and all your expensive appliances will also need maintenance over the years. So, before you decide to buy, take stock of your overall financial health.

If you have good credit and a reliable source of employment, lenders will eagerly offer to loan you money. They'll tell you how much you may borrow from them — the maximum that you're qualified to borrow. Just because they offer you that maximum amount, however, doesn't mean you should borrow the maximum.

Buying a home without considering your other monthly expenditures and long-term goals may cause you to end up with a home that dictates much of your future spending. Have you considered, for example, how much you need to save monthly to reach your retirement goals? How about the amount you want to spend on recreation and entertainment?

If you want to continue your current lifestyle, you have to be honest with yourself about how much you can really afford to spend as a homeowner. First-time homebuyers in particular run into financial trouble when they don't understand their current spending. Buying a home can be a wise decision, but it can also be a huge burden. And you can buy all sorts of nifty things for a home. Some people prop up their spending habits with credit cards — a dangerous practice.

Don't let your home control your financial future. Before you buy a property or agree to a particular mortgage, be sure you can afford to do so — be especially careful not to ignore your retirement planning (if you hope to someday retire). Start by reading Chapter 2.

Another factor to consider when you decide how much you should borrow is that most lenders require you to purchase *mortgage insurance* if your down payment is less than 20 percent of your home's purchase price. Mortgage insurance protects the lender from getting stuck with a property that may be worth less than the mortgage you owe, in the event that you default on your loan. On a moderate-sized loan, mortgage insurance can add hundreds of dollars per year to your payments.

If you have to take mortgage insurance to buy a home with less than 20 percent down, keep an eye on your home's value and your loan balance. Over time, the value of your property should appreciate and your loan balance should decrease as you make monthly payments. After your mortgage represents 80 percent or less of the market value of the home, you can get rid of the mortgage insurance (doing so entails contacting your lender and usually requires you to pay for an appraisal).

What if you have so much money that you can afford to make more than a 20 percent to 25 percent down payment? How much should you put down then? (This problem doesn't usually arise — most buyers, especially first-time buyers, struggle to get a 20 percent to 25 percent down payment together.) The answer depends on what else you can or want to do with the money. If you're considering other investment opportunities, determine whether you can expect to earn a higher rate of return on those other investments versus the pretax cost of the interest rate that you'd pay on the mortgage.

During the past century, stock market and real estate investors have enjoyed average annual returns of around 9 percent per year. So, if you borrow mortgage money at around 4 percent to 6 percent, in the long term you should come out several percent ahead if you use the money you would have put toward a larger down payment to invest in such growth investments. You aren't guaranteed, of course, that your investments will earn 9 percent yearly. (Past returns don't guarantee the future.) And don't forget that all investments come with risk.

If you prefer to put down just 20 percent or 25 percent and invest more money elsewhere, that's fine. Just don't keep the extra money (beyond an emergency reserve) under the mattress, in a savings account, in a money market fund, or in bonds that pay less interest than your mortgage costs you in interest. Invest in stocks, real estate, or a small business. Otherwise, you don't have a chance at earning a higher return than the cost of your mortgage and, therefore, you'll be better off paying down your mortgage.

Property Type Selection

If you're ready to buy a home, you must make some decisions about what and where to buy. If you grew up in the suburbs, your image of a home may include the traditional single-family home with a lawn, kids, and family pets. But single-family homes, of course, aren't the only or even the main type of residential housing in many areas, especially in some higher-cost, urban neighborhoods. Other common types of higher-density ("shared") housing include the following:

- **Condominiums:** Condominiums are generally apartment-style units that are stacked on top of and adjacent to one another. Many condo buildings were originally apartments that were converted — through the sale of ownership of separate units — into condos. When you purchase a condominium, you purchase a specific unit, as well as a share of the common areas (for example, the pool, landscaping, elevators, furnaces, garbage systems, entry and hallways, laundry room, and so on).

- **Townhouses:** A townhouse is an attached or row home. Think of a townhouse as a cross between a condominium and a single-family house. Townhouses are like condos because they're attached (generally sharing walls and a roof), and they're like houses because they're often two-story buildings that come with a small yard.

- **Cooperatives:** Cooperatives (usually called *co-ops*) resemble apartment and condominium buildings. When you buy a share in a cooperative, you own a share of the entire building, including some living space. Unlike in a condo, you generally need to get approval from the cooperative association if you want to remodel or rent your unit to a tenant. In some co-ops, you must even gain approval from the association for the sale of your unit to a proposed buyer. Co-ops are generally much harder to get loans for, and to sell, so don't buy one unless you get a good deal and can easily get a loan.

 All types of shared housing in the preceding list offer two potential advantages:

- **This type of housing generally gives you more living space for your dollars.** This value makes sense because with a single-family home, a good chunk of the property's cost is for the land that the home sits on. Land is good for decks, recreation, and playing children, but you don't live "in" it the way you do with your home. Shared housing maximizes living space for the housing dollars you spend.

- **In many situations, you're not personally responsible for general maintenance.** Instead, the homeowner's association (which you pay into) takes care of it. If you don't have the time, energy, or desire to keep up a property, shared housing can make sense. Shared housing units may also give you access to recreation facilities, such as a pool, meeting and party rooms, tennis courts, and exercise equipment.

So, why doesn't everyone purchase shared housing? Well, as investments, single-family homes generally outperform other housing types. Shared housing is easier to build (and to overbuild) — and the greater supply tends to keep prices from rising as much. Single-family homes tend to attract more potential buyers — most people, when they can afford it, prefer a stand-alone house, especially for the increased privacy.

If you can afford a smaller single-family house instead of a larger shared-housing unit and don't shudder at the thought of maintaining a house, buy the single-family house. Shared housing makes more sense for people who don't want to deal with building maintenance and who value the security of living in a larger building with other people. Keep in mind that shared housing prices tend to hold up better in developed urban environments. If possible, avoid shared housing units in suburban areas where the availability of developable land makes building many more units possible, thus increasing the supply of housing and slowing growth in values.

If shared housing interests you, make sure you have the property thoroughly inspected. Also, examine the trend in maintenance fees over time to ensure that these costs are under control. Finally, inspect the minutes of the recent contingency reserve fund meetings so there are no financial, political, or social surprises.

How to Find the Right Property and Location

Some people know where they want to live, so they look at just a handful of properties and then buy. Most people take much more time; finding the right house in a desired area at a fair price can take a lot of time. Buying a home can also entail a lot of compromise when you buy with other family members, particularly spouses.

Be realistic about how long it may take you to get up to speed about different areas and to find a home that meets your various desires. If you're like most people and you have a full-time job that allows only occasional weekends and evenings to look for a house, three to six months is a short time period to settle on an area and actually find and successfully negotiate on a property. Six months to a year isn't unusual or slow. Keep in mind that you're talking about an enormous purchase that you'll come, well, *home* to, daily.

Real estate agents can be a big barrier to taking your time with this monumental decision. Some agents are pushy and want to make a sale and get their commission. Try not to work with such agents as a buyer — they can make you miserable, unhappy, and broke. If necessary, begin your search without an agent to avoid this outside pressure.

Keep an open mind

Before you start your search for a new home, you may have an idea about the type of property and location that interests you or that you think you can afford. You may think, for example, that you can only afford a condominium in the neighbourhood that you want. But if you take the time to check out other communities, you may find another area that meets most of your needs and has affordable single-family homes. You'd never know that, though, if you narrowed down your search too quickly.

Even if you've lived in an area for a while and you think you know it well, look at different types of properties in a variety of locations before you start to narrow down your search. Be open-minded and make sure you know which of your many criteria for a home you *really* care about. You'll likely have to be flexible with some of your preferences.

After you focus on a particular area or neighbourhood, make sure you see the full range of properties available. If you want to spend $600,000 on a home, look at properties that are more expensive. Many times, especially outside of hot markets such as Vancouver and Toronto, real estate sells for less than its listing price, and you may feel comfortable spending a little bit more after you see what you can purchase if you stretch your budget a little bit. Also, if you work with an agent, make sure you don't overlook homes that are for sale by their owners (that is, properties not listed with real estate agents). Otherwise, you may miss out on some good prospects.

Research, research, research

Thinking that you can know what an area is like from anecdotes or from a small number of personal experiences is a mistake. You may have read or heard that someone was mugged in a particular area. That incident doesn't make that area dangerous — or more dangerous than others. *Get the facts.* Anecdotes and people's perceptions often aren't accurate reflections of the facts. Check out the following key items in an area:

- **Amenities:** Hopefully, you don't spend all your time at work, slaving away to make your monthly mortgage payment. Hopefully, you have time to use parks, sports and recreation facilities, and so on. You can drive around the neighbourhood you're interested in to get a sense of these attractions. Most real estate agents just love to show off their favourite neighbourhoods. Websites for cities and towns detail what they have to offer and where you can find it.

- **Schools:** If you have kids, you care about this issue a lot. Unfortunately, many people make snap judgments about school quality without doing their homework. Visit the schools and don't blindly rely on test scores. Talk to parents and teachers and discover what goes on at the schools.

  If you don't have or want school-age children, you may be tempted to say, "What the heck does it matter about the quality of the schools?" You need to care about the schools because even if you don't have kids, the quality of the local schools and whether they're improving or faltering affects property values. Consider schooling issues even if they're not important to you because they can affect the resale value of your property.

- **Property taxes:** What will your property taxes be? Property tax rates vary from community to community. Check with the town's assessment office or with a good real estate agent.

- **Crime:** Call the local police department or visit your public library to get the facts on crime. Cities and towns keep all sorts of crime statistics for neighbourhoods — use them.

- **Future development:** Check with the planning department in towns that you're considering living in to find out what types of new development and major renovations are in the works. Planning people may also be aware of problems in particular areas.

- **Catastrophic risks:** Are the neighbourhoods you're considering susceptible to major risks, such as floods, tornadoes, mudslides, fires, or earthquakes? Although homeowner's insurance can protect you financially, consider how you may deal with such catastrophes emotionally. Insurance eases only the financial pain of a home loss. All areas have some risk, and a home in the safest of areas can burn to the ground. Although you can't eliminate all risks, you can at least educate yourself about the potential catastrophic risks in various areas.

If you're new to an area or you don't have a handle on an area's risks, try a number of different sources. Knowledgeable and honest real estate agents may help, but you can also dig for primary information. For example, Environment and Climate Change Canada, as well as the Public Safety Canada office, can help you investigate potential flooding and earthquake risks in the area you're considering.

You can find out more at `http://weather.gc.ca`.
Insurance companies and agencies can also tell you
what they know about risks in particular areas.

Understand market value

Over many months, you'll look at perhaps dozens of properties for sale. Use these viewings as an opportunity to find out
what specific homes are worth. The listing price isn't what a
house is worth — it may be, but odds are it's not. Property
that's priced to sell usually does just that: It sells. Properties
left on the market are often overpriced. The listing price on
such properties may reflect what an otherwise greedy or unin-
formed seller and his agent hope that some fool will pay.

Of the properties that you see, keep track of the
prices that they end up selling for. (Good agents can
provide this information.) Properties usually sell for
less than the listed price. Keeping track of selling
prices gives you a good handle on what properties are
really worth and a better sense of what you can afford.

Pound the pavement

After you set your sights on that special home, thoroughly
check out the surroundings — you should know what you're
getting yourself into.

At different times of the day and on different days of the week, go back to the neighbourhood in which the property is located. Knock on a few doors and meet your potential neighbours. Ask questions. Talk to property owners as well as renters. Because renters don't have a financial stake in the area, they're often more forthcoming with negative information about an area.

7

Assessing Your Appetite for Small Business

Many people dream about running their own companies —
and for good reason. If you start your own business, you can
pursue something that you're passionate about, *and* you have
more control over how you do things. Plus, successful business
owners can reap major economic bounties.

But tales of entrepreneurs becoming multimillionaires
focus attention on the financial rewards without revealing the
challenges and costs associated with being in charge. Consider
what your company has to do well to survive and succeed in
the competitive business world:

- Develop products and services that customers
  will purchase.

- Price your offerings properly and promote them.
- Deal with the competition.
- Manage the accounting and tax reporting.
- Interpret lease contracts and evaluate office space.
- Stay current with changes in your field.
- Hire, train, manage, motivate, and retain good employees.

Business owners also face personal and emotional challenges, which rarely get any airtime among all the glory of the rags-to-riches tales of multimillionaire entrepreneurs. Major health problems, divorces, fights and lawsuits among family members who are in business together, the loss of friends, and even suicides have been attributed to the passions of business owners who are consumed with winning or become overwhelmed by their failures. And then there are the untold numbers of businesses that never get off the ground. Or they do, but then fail, often stunningly quickly.

An artisan coffee roaster catches on with neighbourhood caffeine enthusiasts, talks her way into being carried by one-off specialty shops, manages to get placed on eye-level shelves of the nation's big supermarket chains, and eventually is bought out by a food-and-beverage global conglomerate. That's just the kind of success story the media loves. So, the news gets zapped all over the Internet, covered on the front page of the newspaper, chatted about on the radio, and talked up at the end of TV broadcasts as a feel-good story. The founder gets invited to share her views with magazines, speak to entrepreneur and business associations, and maybe even give the occasional lecture at noted business schools.

Many folks who heard this raw-coffee-beans-to-riches story would be hard-put not to — after kicking themselves in the hindquarters for not having started importing and roasting beans in their basements themselves — marvel how easy it is to succeed at small business. They'll want to rush off and launch themselves — and their savings — into turning that little idea they'd always had in the back of their minds into the next very-big thing.

But what the media reports *don't* include is just how many other entrepreneurs had the same idea; pursued it with an equal amount of energy, effort, and smarts; and were either still, well, "grinding it out" in their spare bedrooms or had long ceased to be in business. A great number of fortuitous events have to occur for any business, no matter how terrific the idea or talented and dedicated the founders, to succeed. Fortunate timing and helpful breaks — often a long string of them — are usually part of the untold story of any small business success story. To put it in perspective? When asked what he attributed the success of the Rolling Stones to, even Sir Mick Jagger's first response was "Luck!" This isn't meant to scare you, but you do need to be realistic about starting your own business.

This chapter helps you assess whether starting a company fits with your goals and aptitude. It also presents numerous small business investment options.

A Test of Your Entrepreneurial IQ

The keys to success and enjoyment as an entrepreneur vary as much as the businesses do. But if you can answer *yes* to most of the following questions, you probably have the qualities and perspective needed to succeed as a small business owner:

- **Are you a self-starter? Do you like challenges? Are you persistent? Are you willing to do research to solve problems?** Most of the time, running your own business isn't glamorous, especially in the early years. You have many details to remember and many things to do. Success in business is the result of doing lots of little things well. If you're accustomed to working for large organizations where much of the day is spent attending meetings and keeping up on office politics and gossip, with little accountability, running your own business may come as a bit of a shock at first.

- **Do you value independence and self-control?** Particularly in the early days of your business, you need to enjoy working on your own. When you leave a company environment and work on your own, you give up a lot of socializing. Of course, if you work in an unpleasant environment or with people you don't really enjoy socializing with, venturing out on your own may be a plus.

If you're a people person, many businesses offer lots of contact. But you must recognize the difference between socializing for fun with coworkers and the often more demanding and goal-oriented networking with business contacts and customers.

- **Can you develop a commitment to an idea, a product, or a principle?** If you work 50 hours per week over 50 weeks per year, you'll work 2,500 hours per year. If the product, service, or cause you're pursuing doesn't excite you and you can't motivate others to work hard for you, you're going to have a *long* year.

One of the worst reasons to start your own business is solely for the pursuit of great financial riches. Yes, if you're good at what you do and you know how to market your services or products, you may make more money working for yourself. But for most people, money isn't enough of a motivation, and many people make the same or less money on their own than they did working for a company.

- **Are you willing to make financial sacrifices and live a reduced lifestyle before and during your early entrepreneurial years?** "Live like a student before and during the start-up of your small business" was the advice that one business school professor gave a student before he started his business. With most businesses, you expend money during the start-up years and likely have a reduced income compared to the income you receive while working for a company. You also have to buy your own benefits.

  To make your entrepreneurial dream a reality, you need to live within your means both before and after you start your business. But if running your own business really makes you happy, sacrificing expensive vacations, overpriced luxury cars, the latest designer clothing, and $4 lattes at the corner cafe shouldn't be too painful.

- **Do you recognize that when you run your own business, you still have to report to bosses?** Besides the allure of huge profits, the other reason some people mistakenly go into business for themselves is that they're tired of working for other people. Obnoxious, evil bosses can make anyone want to become an entrepreneur.

When you run your own business, you may have customers and other people to please who are unpleasant to deal with. Fortunately, even the worst customers usually can't make your life anywhere near as miserable as the worst bosses. (And if you have enough customers, you can simply decide not to do business with such misfits.) You also still have to deal with a large number of other people who can — and likely often will — leave you stressed and headache-ridden, not all that different from how a boss or two might have left you feeling on a bad day at the office. This includes suppliers, contractors, bankers, accountants, lawyers, and regulators.

- **Can you withstand rejection, naysayers, and negative feedback?** "I thought every *no* that I got when trying to raise my funding brought me one step closer to a *yes*," says an entrepreneur. Unless you come from an entrepreneurial family, don't expect your parents to endorse your "risky, crazy" behaviour. Even other entrepreneurs can ridicule your good ideas. Two entrepreneurial friends were critical of each other's ideas, yet both have succeeded.

Some people (especially parents) simply think that working for a giant company makes you safer and more secure (which, of course, is a myth because corporations can — and regularly do — lay off employees in a snap). It's also easier for them to say to their friends and neighbours that you're a big manager at a well-known corporation (such as Loblaw, Bell, Tim Hortons, or one of the big banks) than to explain that you're working on some kooky business idea out of your spare bedroom. How secure do you think the many former employees of Nortel, Research in Motion, and Sears feel now about having lost their jobs at their former large companies?

- **Are you able to identify your shortcomings and hire or align yourself with people and organizations that complement your skills and expertise?** To be a successful entrepreneur, you need to be a bit of a jack-of-all-trades: marketer, accountant, customer service representative, administrative assistant, and so on. Unless you get lots of investor capital, which is rare for a true start-up, you can't afford to hire help in the early months, or perhaps even years, of your business.

Partnering with or buying certain services or products rather than trying to do everything yourself may make sense for you. And over time, if your business grows and succeeds, you should be able to afford to hire more help. If you can be honest with yourself and surround and partner yourself with people whose skills and expertise complement yours, you can build a winning team.

- **Do you deal well with ambiguity? Do you believe in yourself?** When you're on your own, determining whether you're on the right track is difficult. Some days, things don't go well — and such days are much harder to take flying solo. Therefore, being confident, optimistic, and able to work around obstacles are necessary skills.

- **Do you understand why you started the business or organization and how you personally define success?** Many business entrepreneurs define success by such measures as sales revenue, profits, number of branch offices and employees, and so on. These are fine measures, but other organizations, particularly nonprofits, have other measures. For example, the Sierra Club of Canada seeks to "develop a diverse, well-trained grassroots network working to protect the integrity of our global ecosystems." Money is necessary for the Sierra Club to accomplish its purpose, but such a cause-focused organization has a "bottom line" that's very different from that of a for-profit organization.

- **Can you accept lack of success in the early years of building your business?** A few, rare businesses are instant hits, but most businesses take time to build momentum — it may take years, perhaps even decades. Some successful corporate people suffer from anxiety when they go out on their own and encounter the inevitable struggles and lack of tangible success as they build their companies.

Don't be deterred by the questions that you can't answer in the affirmative. A perfect entrepreneur doesn't exist. Part of succeeding in business is knowing what you can and can't do and then finding creative ways (or people) to help you achieve your goals.

Small Business Investment Options

The only thing limiting the ways you can make money with a small business is your imagination. Choosing the option that best meets your needs is similar to choosing investments in other areas, such as real estate or the securities markets. The following sections discuss the major ways you can invest in small business, including what's attractive and not about each option.

Start your own business

Many people of varied backgrounds, interests, and skills achieve success and happiness running their own businesses. Of all your small business options, starting your own business involves the greatest amount of work. Although you can perform this work on a part-time basis in the beginning, most people end up working in their business full-time.

Most people perceive starting a business as the riskiest of all small business investment options. But if you get into a business that uses your skills and expertise, the risk isn't nearly as great as you may think. Suppose, for example, that as a teacher you make $65,000 per year, and now you decide you want to set up your own tutoring service, making a comparable amount of money. If you find through your research that others who perform these services charge $50 per hour, you need to tutor about 30 to 35 or so hours per week, assuming that you work 48 weeks per year. Because you can run this business from your home (which can possibly generate small tax breaks) without purchasing new equipment, your expenses should be minimal. However, you'll have to pay for your benefits and fund your retirement plan yourself.

Instead of leaving your job cold turkey and trying to build your business from scratch, you can start moonlighting as a tutor in the evenings and on the weekend. Over a couple of years, if you can build the tutoring up to 15 hours per week, you're halfway to your goal. If you leave your job and focus all your energies on your tutoring business, getting to 30 to 35 hours per week of billable work shouldn't be a problem. Still think starting a business is risky?

 You can start many businesses with little money by leveraging your existing skills and expertise. If you have the time to devote to building "sweat equity," you can build a valuable company and job. As long as you check out the competition and offer a valued product or service at a reasonable cost, the principal risk with your business is that you won't do a good job marketing what you have to offer. If you can market your skills, you should succeed.

Buy an existing business

If you don't have a specific idea for a business that you want to start but you have business management skills and an ability to improve existing businesses, consider buying an established business. Although you don't have to go through the riskier start-up period if you take this route, you'll likely need more capital to buy a going enterprise.

You also need to be able to deal with potentially sticky personnel and management issues. The history of the organization and the way things work predates your ownership of the business. If you don't like making hard decisions, firing people who don't fit with your plans, and coercing people into changing the way they did things before you arrived on the scene, buying an existing business likely isn't for you. Also realize that some of the good employees may be loyal to the old owner and his style of running the business, so they may split when you arrive.

Some people think that buying an existing business is safer than starting a new one, but buying someone else's business can actually be riskier. You have to put out far more money up front, in the form of a down payment, to buy a business. And if you don't have the ability to run the business and it does poorly, you may lose much more financially. Another risk is that the business may be for sale for a reason — perhaps it's not very profitable, it's in decline, or it's generally a pain in the posterior to operate.

Good businesses that are for sale don't come cheaply. If the business is a success, the current owner has removed the start-up risk from the business, so the price of the business should include a premium to reflect this lack of risk. If you have the capital to buy an established business and the skills to run it, consider going this route.

Invest in someone else's business

If you like the idea of profiting from successful small businesses but you don't want the day-to-day headaches of being responsible for managing the enterprise, you may want to invest in someone else's small business. Although this route may seem easier, fewer people are actually cut out to be investors in other people's businesses.

Choose to invest for the right reasons

Consider investing in someone else's business if you meet the following criteria:

- **You have sufficient assets.** You need enough assets so that what you invest in small, privately held companies is a small portion (20 percent or less) of your total financial assets.

- **You can afford to lose what you invest.** Unlike investing in a diversified stock fund (see Chapter 5), you may lose all your investment when you invest in a small, privately held company.

- **You're astute at evaluating financial statements and business strategies.** Investing in a small, privately held company has a lot in common with investing in a publicly traded firm. One major difference is that private firms aren't required to produce comprehensive, audited financial statements that adhere to certain accounting principles the way that public companies are. So, you have a greater risk of not receiving sufficient or accurate information when you evaluate a small, private firm. (There are also liquidity differences; with a small, private company, you may not be able to sell out when you want and at a fair current price.)

Putting money into your own business (or someone else's) can be a high-risk — but potentially high-return — investment.

The best options are those that you understand well. If you hear about a great business idea or company from someone you know and trust, do your research and make your best judgment. That company or idea may be a terrific investment.

Before you invest, ask to see a copy of the business plan. Thoroughly check out the people running the business. Talk to others who don't have a stake in the investment; you can benefit from their comments and concerns. But don't forget that many a wise person has rained on the parade of what turned out to be a terrific business idea.

Avoid investing mistakes

Although some people are extra careful when they invest other people's money, others aren't. For example, many small business owners seek investors' money for the wrong reasons, including the following:

- They're impatient and perhaps don't understand the feasibility of making do with a small amount of capital (a process called *bootstrapping*).

- They need money because they're in financial trouble. Take the small furniture retailer that conducted a stock offering to raise money. On the surface, everything seemed fine, and the company made it onto the *Inc. 500* list of fast-growing small companies. But it turns out that the company wanted to issue stock because it expanded too quickly and didn't sell enough merchandise to cover its high overhead. The company ended up in bankruptcy.

Here's another problem with small businesses that seek investors: Many small business owners take more risk and do less up-front planning and homework with other people's money. In fact, many well-intentioned people fail at their businesses.

Consider the MBA from a top business school — you can call him Jacob — who convinced an investor to put up about $300,000 to purchase a small manufacturing company. Jacob put a small amount of his own money into the business and immediately blew about $100,000 on a fancy computer-scheduling and order-entry system. Jacob wasn't interested much in sales (a job that the previous owner managed), so he also hired a sales manager. The sales manager he hired was a disaster — many of the frontline salespeople fled to competitors, taking key customers with them. He tried to cut costs, but doing so hurt the quality and timeliness of the company's products. By the time Jacob came to his senses, it was too late. The business dissolved, and the investor lost everything.

About the Authors

Eric Tyson is an internationally acclaimed and best-selling personal finance author and speaker. He has worked with and taught people from all financial situations, so he knows the financial concerns and questions of real folks. Despite having an MBA from the Stanford Graduate School of Business and a BS in economics and biology from Yale University, Eric remains a master of "keeping it simple."

He figured out how to pursue his dream after working as a management consultant to Fortune 500 financial service firms. Eric took his inside knowledge of the banking, investment, and insurance industries and committed himself to making personal financial management accessible to all.

He is the author of several national best-selling financial books in Wiley's *For Dummies* series, including books on personal finance, investing, mutual funds, home buying (coauthor), and real estate investing (coauthor). His *Personal Finance For Dummies* (Wiley) won the Benjamin Franklin Award for best business book of the year. An accomplished personal finance writer, his "Investors' Guide" syndicated column, distributed by King Features, is read by millions nationally, and he was an award-winning columnist for the *San Francisco Examiner*.

Eric's work has been featured and quoted in hundreds of local and national publications, including *Newsweek, The Wall Street Journal, Los Angeles Times, Chicago Tribune, Forbes,*

Kiplinger's Personal Finance, Parenting, Money, and *Bottom Line/ Personal;* on NBC's *Today Show,* ABC, CNBC, PBS's *Nightly Business Report,* CNN, and FOX; and on CBS national radio, NPR's *Marketplace Money,* and Bloomberg Radio.

Eric's website is www.erictyson.com.

Tony Martin has always had an innate understanding of money. Instead of getting his (tiny) allowance paid out to him weekly in shiny coins like his brothers did, he asked his mom to keep track of how much he was owed.

After emerging from Queen's University business school with a BCom, despite a transcript that listed courses such as "Electronic Music" and "The Philosophy of Religion," Tony set off to see the world. On his return, he joined CBC radio, and ever since, he has been helping people understand the world of money.

Noticing there was an absence of sound, easy-to-read financial guides for Canadians that were also easy to implement, Tony approached the publishers of the *For Dummies* series with the idea of writing a Canadian-centric version of *Personal Finance For Dummies.* And thus, the first non-U.S. *For Dummies* title was born, with Tony becoming the first Canadian — and first ever non-American — *For Dummies* author. In addition to coauthoring the national Canadian best-seller *Personal Finance For Canadians For Dummies,* Tony and Eric also worked together to write the best-selling *Investing For Canadians For Dummies.*

For over a decade, Tony's widely read column "Me and My Money" appeared in the *Globe and Mail*'s weekend personal finance section. He was also the investing columnist for *Report on Business Magazine.* His work has been featured in many leading publications, including MoneySense, IE Money, *Profit, Reader's Digest,* and *Canadian Business.* Tony is a frequent commentator and speaker on personal finance and investing and regularly appears on television and radio, including BNN CBC Radio, CBC Television, BCC, and TVOntario.

Tony has been instrumental in the design and development of many leading online resources, including an interactive investor training program using simulated stock market transactions. He also was editorial head for i|money.com, Canada's first financial website, which later became the content for Canoe.ca. He has worked extensively as a communications consultant, editorial advisor, and educator. His clients include Bank of America, Barrick, BMO, Business Development Bank of Canada, Fidelity, Geico, IBM, Integra, Manulife, The Principal Group, Scotiabank, Sun Life Financial, TD Bank, and VISA Canada.

Tony is also an accomplished and engaging teacher, lecturer, and management trainer. He leads courses across the country on finance and accounting, as well as speaking and presenting, business writing, writing for the web, public speaking and presenting, negotiating, and conflict resolution for national management training leaders, as well as many major companies and organizations, including Shoppers Drug Mart, Siemens, the Ontario Government, and Ontario Power Corp.

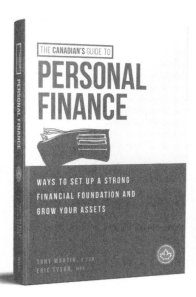
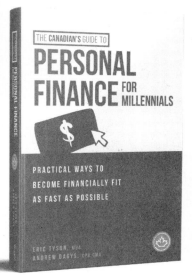

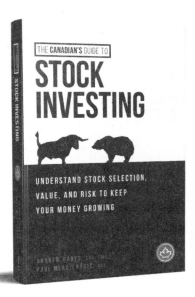

THE CANADIAN'S GUIDE TO
STOCK INVESTING

UNDERSTAND STOCK SELECTION,
VALUE, AND RISK TO KEEP
YOUR MONEY GROWING

978-1-119-61189-9

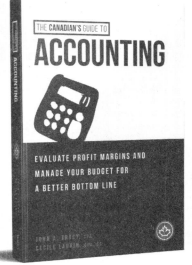

THE CANADIAN'S GUIDE TO
ACCOUNTING

EVALUATE PROFIT MARGINS AND
MANAGE YOUR BUDGET FOR
A BETTER BOTTOM LINE

978-1-119-60934-6